ROUTLEDGE LIBRARY EDITIONS:
LIBRARY AND INFORMATION SCIENCE

Volume 40

THE FUTURE OF RESOURCE SHARING

THE FUTURE OF RESOURCE SHARING

Edited by
SHIRLEY K. BAKER AND MARY E. JACKSON

LONDON AND NEW YORK

First published in 1995 by The Haworth Press, Inc.

This edition first published in 2020
by Routledge
2 Park Square, Milton Park, Abingdon, Oxon OX14 4RN

and by Routledge
52 Vanderbilt Avenue, New York, NY 10017

Routledge is an imprint of the Taylor & Francis Group, an informa business

© 1995 The Haworth Press, Inc.

All rights reserved. No part of this book may be reprinted or reproduced or utilised in any form or by any electronic, mechanical, or other means, now known or hereafter invented, including photocopying and recording, or in any information storage or retrieval system, without permission in writing from the publishers.

Trademark notice: Product or corporate names may be trademarks or registered trademarks, and are used only for identification and explanation without intent to infringe.

British Library Cataloguing in Publication Data
A catalogue record for this book is available from the British Library

ISBN: 978-0-367-34616-4 (Set)
ISBN: 978-0-429-34352-0 (Set) (ebk)
ISBN: 978-0-367-36071-9 (Volume 40) (hbk)
ISBN: 978-0-367-36089-4 (Volume 40) (pbk)
ISBN: 978-0-429-34374-2 (Volume 40) (ebk)

Publisher's Note
The publisher has gone to great lengths to ensure the quality of this reprint but points out that some imperfections in the original copies may be apparent.

Disclaimer
The publisher has made every effort to trace copyright holders and would welcome correspondence from those they have been unable to trace.

The Future of Resource Sharing

Shirley K. Baker
Mary E. Jackson
Editors

The Haworth Press, Inc.
New York · London

The Future of Resource Sharing has also been published as *Journal of Library Administration,* Volume 21, Numbers 1/2 1995.

© 1995 by The Haworth Press, Inc. All rights reserved. No part of this work may be reproduced or utilized in any form or by any means, electronic or mechanical, including photocopying, microfilm and recording, or by any information storage and retrieval system, without permission in writing from the publisher. Printed in the United States of America.

The development, preparation, and publication of this work has been undertaken with great care. However, the publisher, employees, editors, and agents of The Haworth Press and all imprints of The Haworth Press, Inc., including The Haworth Medical Press and Pharmaceutical Products Press, are not responsible for any errors contained herein or for consequences that may ensue from use of materials or information contained in this work. Opinions expressed by the author(s) are not necessarily those of The Haworth Press, Inc.

The Haworth Press, Inc., 10 Alice Street, Binghamton, NY 13904-1580 USA

Library of Congress Cataloging-in-Publication Data

The future of resource sharing / Shirley K. Baker, Mary E. Jackson, editors.
     p. cm.
     Includes bibliographical references (p.) and index.
     ISBN 1-56024-773-8 (alk. paper)
     1. Interlibrary loans–United States. 2. Library cooperation–United States. 3. Research libraries–United States. 4. Academic libraries–United States. I. Baker, Shirley K. II. Jackson, Mary E.
Z713.5.U6F87 1995
025.6'2–dc20   95-35946
                                                                  CIP

The Future of Resource Sharing

CONTENTS

Introduction   1
  Shirley K. Baker

The Research University's Dilemma: Resource Sharing
  and Research in a Transinstitutional Environment   5
  Lawrence Dowler

Resource Sharing: The Public University Library's
  Imperative   27
  Nancy L. Eaton

Real Access as the Paradigm of the Nineties   39
  Paul H. Mosher

Scholarly Publishing, Copyright, and the Future
  of Resource Sharing   49
  William Gray Potter

Future of Resource Sharing in Research Libraries   67
  Jutta Reed-Scott

Resource Sharing and Prices   77
  Malcolm Getz

The Future Using an Integrated Approach:
  The OhioLINK Experience   109
  Phyllis O'Connor
  Susan Wehmeyer
  Susan Weldon

Impact of Holdings on Resource Sharing   121
  Julie Wessling

Commercial Document Delivery: The Academic Library's
Perspective   133
> *Nancy S. Hewison*
> *Vicki J. Killion*
> *Suzanne M. Ward*

System Architecture and Networking Issues in Implementing
the North American Interlibrary Loan and Document
Delivery (NAILDD) Initiative   145
> *Clifford A. Lynch*

The Future of Document Delivery: A Vendor's Perspective   169
> *Melissa Stockton*
> *Martha Whittaker*

Staff and Training Issues: Optimizing the Potential
of Library Partnerships   183
> *Jack Siggins*

The Future of Resource Sharing: The Role of the Association
of Research Libraries   193
> *Mary E. Jackson*

Index   203

Introduction

Shirley K. Baker

The volume you hold in your hand addresses a key issue for libraries today: surviving in an age of interdependence. Increasingly, individual libraries must act as if each is a part of a *world library*. Instead of being self-sufficient, each library must find ways to put materials from the *world library* into the hands of its own patrons and must stand ready to supply materials from its own collection to others, quickly and cost-effectively.

Resource sharing in libraries means both cooperative collection development (as reflected in the Farmington Plan agreements or the recent Association of Research Libraries' Distributed North American Collections effort) and interlibrary loan, or the movement of materials among libraries and other suppliers in response to users' needs. This volume refers primarily but not exclusively to the interlibrary loan aspects of resource sharing.

Interlibrary loan as a library function is a little more than one hundred years old. Initially, a director might write a letter to the director of another library, requesting the loan of a particular book for use by a senior scholar. As information about the holdings of libraries became available in book catalogs and union lists, the volume of requests grew and the need for standardized methods and codes of conduct became apparent. (Mary E. Jackson has documented early mentions of interlibrary loan and the history of standardized forms.)[1]

Shirley K. Baker is Dean of University Libraries at Washington University in St. Louis, MO.

[Haworth co-indexing entry note]: "Introduction." Baker, Shirley K. Co-published simultaneously in *Journal of Library Administration* (The Haworth Press, Inc.) Vol. 21, No. 1/2, 1995, pp. 1-3; and *The Future of Resource Sharing* (ed: Shirley K. Baker, and Mary E. Jackson) The Haworth Press, Inc., 1995, pp. 1-3. Multiple copies of this article/chapter may be purchased from The Haworth Document Delivery Center [1-800-342-9678; 9:00 a.m. - 5:00 p.m. (EST)].

© 1995 by The Haworth Press, Inc. All rights reserved.

THE FUTURE OF RESOURCE SHARING

In the last two decades, with explosive growth in the volume of publishing, the ubiquitous presence of photocopy machines, the advent of electronic catalogs of thousands of libraries, and the creation of electronic interlibrary messaging systems, the volume and character of the movement of materials has changed dramatically. What was once a slow process of requesting bound volumes from, primarily, a few large libraries, became a speedy method of obtaining materials or copies from a multitude of sources.

Many small libraries found themselves supplying far more than they borrowed, as it became apparent that small libraries could respond more quickly than complex and overwhelmed research libraries. Many large libraries, still facing many requests to lend, began to impose charges for loans, to recover costs and to discourage use. Cost-recovery and for-profit suppliers, especially for copies of journal articles, began to appear. Consortia, guaranteeing preferential treatment and often cost avoidance, became common, until, by 1992, the average research library had eight such agreements.[2]

As the volume of interlibrary traffic increased, the practice lost its "for scholars only" aura. The American Library Association's *National Interlibrary Loan Code*, the code governing interchange among libraries, became less restrictive. The code was revised in 1980[3] and again in 1993.[4] With each revision, the recommendations on what might be lent and for whom became broader and looser, reflecting the evolution of resource sharing among libraries from exception to mainstream.

We are now at a turning point in resource sharing. What has been traditionally called *interlibrary loan* is often not a loan and is frequently not interlibrary. Increasingly, electronic supply of documents replaces the shipping of hard copy. Yet significant traffic in traditional materials remains and will continue for the foreseeable future. Our short term need is to address the many issues involved in making the current system work significantly better while we prepare for the future. This collection of essays serves as a reader on the current issues and future directions.

This volume signifies the movement of resource sharing from a marginal to a key issue for even the largest research libraries. As is evident from these essays, resource sharing has captured the atten-

Introduction 3

tion of library directors. Many have come to see beyond lending as a nuisance and borrowing an embarrassment; they have come to view their ability to place materials from around the world into the hands of their users as a key measure of success for their libraries.

Essays in this collection explore the critical questions for making resource sharing work in today's world. They bring historical perspective, explore the future, and report from multiple perspectives. Economic decision models, consortial arrangements, copyright dilemmas, and the possibilities of technology are explored. Finally, a national project to revamp interlibrary loan and document delivery is described and future directions posited.

NOTES

1. "Standardization of the Interlibrary Loan Request," by Mary E. Jackson, in *Research Access Through Technology*, AMS Press, New York, 1989.

2. Unpublished data collected by the Association of Research Libraries in 1992.

3. *National Interlibrary Loan Code*, ALA, Chicago, 1980.

4. "National Interlibrary Loan Code, 1993," *RQ*, v. 33, no. 4, Summer 1994, pp. 477-79.

The Research University's Dilemma: Resource Sharing and Research in a Transinstitutional Environment

Lawrence Dowler

Rising publication costs and declining financial resources have resulted in renewed interest among librarians in resource sharing. Although the idea of sharing resources is not new, there is a sense of urgency not seen in the past. For many libraries, obtaining even basic works has become a challenge and frequency of use is playing a greater part in library decisions, ranging from where books are shelved (on or off site), which books go to the head of the queue for preservation, and even which books are acquired. Driven by rising publication costs and static and often shrinking budgets, librarians are embracing resource sharing as an idea whose time may finally have come.

As the titles of the essays in this volume clearly suggest, librarians do not question the need to share resources (if they ever did), but appear increasingly concerned with how to do so effectively. "Inter-library loan," "document delivery," "technical issues," "intellectual property rights," "the costs of sharing and the staffing and training for these services," are issues of *how* to share resources. The locus of concern, then, is how to create an infrastruc-

---

Lawrence Dowler is Associate Librarian of Public Services, Harvard College Library, Harvard University, Cambridge, MA.

[Haworth co-indexing entry note]: "The Research University's Dilemma: Resource Sharing and Research in a Transinstitutional Environment." Dowler, Lawrence. Co-published simultaneously in *Journal of Library Administration* (The Haworth Press, Inc.) Vol. 21, No. 1/2, 1995, pp. 5-26; and *The Future of Resource Sharing* (ed: Shirley K. Baker, and Mary E. Jackson) The Haworth Press, Inc., 1995, pp. 5-26. Multiple copies of this article/chapter may be purchased from The Haworth Document Delivery Center [1-800-342-9678; 9:00 a.m. - 5:00 p.m. (EST)].

© 1995 by The Haworth Press, Inc. All rights reserved.

THE FUTURE OF RESOURCE SHARING

ture to share resources efficiently, rather than what resources will be available to share.

Emerging technologies, especially digital imaging technologies, draw librarians toward a vision of vastly improved access and information retrieval. In short, there is a classic push-pull model at work. Rising cost and shrinking resources compel libraries to design strategies and systems to provide the sources they can no longer afford; new technology exerts a powerful pull toward access and retrieval as the principal solution to our common dilemma. Access has replaced ownership as our guide, and, on the surface at least, sharing appears to have replaced competition as the reigning principal of librarianship.

The issue, however, is not whether or how to build mechanisms to share resources, but how to build collections and information resources that can be shared. As one observer puts it, "The chief economic challenge we now face is how to apply the new technologies in a way that preserves the value and disciplines that made them possible in the first place."[1] How can we support research in an environment that is no longer defined by local resources, and what role should individual research libraries play in supporting it? This is a question librarians are not empowered to answer, thus they have tended to seek solutions that mirror parts of the existing system. What is needed, however, is a new model for acquiring and preserving the sources that will be needed for research and a new system for supporting it.

RESOURCE SHARING AS COOPERATIVE COLLECTION BUILDING

There can be little doubt that whatever broad vision informed pioneering efforts to share resources, the driving motive behind resource sharing today is rising costs and diminished library resources. Few institutions have been able to maintain acquisitions at the same level as the past and the explosion in the number and variety of publications means that all research libraries, no matter how well funded, are acquiring an ever smaller portion of the world's publications. In his 1981 annual report on the University of Pennsylvania Libraries, Richard De Gennaro used statistical tables to demonstrate the inexorable trend between rising book production and declining library materials budgets. Between 1971 and 1981, the annual number of volumes added to the University of Pennsylvania Libraries declined 27 percent as the cost of books published in the United States increased tenfold and the annual production of science and technology books in the United States registered nearly a fivefold increase.[2] Clearly, the production and cost of information and the library's ability to collect and organize it were moving in opposite directions.

A little more than a decade later, conditions had deteriorated even further. According to the Association of Research Libraries, libraries continue to spend more dollars for fewer resources. During the period 1985-86 to 1992-93, "both total expenditures for serials and the price per serial subscription almost doubled for ARL libraries."[3] From 1986 to 1993, serials expenditures have nearly doubled while subscriptions have declined 5% and this trend is likely to continue for the foreseeable future. And while serials are claiming more and more of library materials budgets, the share for monographs is also falling. By 1993, ARL members purchased 23% fewer monographs and paid 16% more. Extrapolating from this data, Kendon Stubbs observes that by the year 2000 libraries may be acquiring only half of the new books they acquired in 1986.[4]

Brian Hawkins paints an even darker picture. "Unless something dramatic is done quickly," says Hawkins,

> we have the potential of losing our society's ability to capture the information that chronicles and documents our civilization. If these same trends continue, by the year 2026, the acquisitions budgets of our finest libraries will only have 20% of the buying power they had forty five years earlier. It should be noted that even this dire outcome assumes the unlikely probability that universities will be able to afford to continue to fund libraries at more than twice the rate of inflation.[5]

It is not surprising that early efforts to share resources focused on cooperative collection development. Charles Osburn's critical assessment of the comprehensive humanities-based model of collection development, did not suggest jettisoning less used research materials. Instead, he argued for a two tiered collection development plan: "One plan, whose rationale is service to the identifiable needs of the immediate constituency; and a second-stage plan, whose rationale is the integration of local development into the national systems of resource sharing in support of the long-range national academic research effort."[6] Cooperation, then, would come to the rescue of research by providing for the resources that individual universities and their libraries could no longer afford.

The declining ability to acquire a significant portion of the world's publications is creating a shift in the concept of the library as a warehouse of print-based collections to the idea of the library as the point of access to needed information. "A library's holdings," writes Lucy Siefert Wegner, "will be defined by access, not by possession. Much of the library's material will be delivered in electronic form, or printed on demand."[7] In this new paradigm libraries can not be expected to support research from their own collections. Ownership of collections and the notion of self-sufficiency give way to cooperation and resource sharing. Clearly, cost is the engine driving this paradigm shift. It is not just the cost of acquiring materials, but the cost of processing, shelving, preserving, and housing books that makes access such an attractive alternative to possession.[8]

These changes, along with improved communications, computerization of administrative functions, fax and digital delivery of articles, even better mail service, are improving the procedures and means for delivering needed information to library patrons. Not surprisingly, interlibrary loan is growing. Since 1986 borrowing transactions per student have increased by 60%,[9] and librarians are more mindful of the discrepancies between the lip service they pay to the importance of interlibrary loans and the reality of inadequate resources devoted to supporting this expanding service.[10]

But there is a dark side to the promise of improved resource sharing. To the extent resource sharing is seen as user driven, that is, perceived by librarians as an acquisitions-on-demand model, there is a danger that this model will be undermined by licensing agreements that could come to dominate the incipient dream of a digital library. In part, this fear reflects the uncertainty of how copyright issues will be resolved in the electronic world,[11] and also raises concerns that the old disparities between the haves and have-nots will continue in the electronic environment, as many believe it did in the print world.[12]

But the current emphasis on resource sharing really begs the question of who in society is responsible for preserving the nation's intellectual and cultural heritage. What Osburn, Mosher and other librarians did was to reject the notion of self-sufficiency in response to the new economic realities; they were reluctant, however, to give up on the idea of comprehensive collections as essential to research.[13] The underlying assumption is that the sum of individual library collection decisions will result in a national system of research sources. This is an issue that goes to the very heart of our understanding and definition of "research" library. Even today we regard large academic and public research libraries as part of the "national" library. And "To national libraries," observe two French librarians, "falls the task of preserving for any given society the record of its past. The question of remembering (and of forgetting) is the fundamental and eternal mission of a national library, the symbolic meeting place of memory and knowledge."[14] The question is, can we continue to expect university research libraries to bear the principal burden of preserving the books and artifacts and, increasingly, electronic information, that comprise our cultural heritage?

THE SELF-SUFFICIENT RESEARCH LIBRARY

There can be little doubt that the idea of the comprehensive or self-sufficient library was a powerful influence on academic research libraries. By the end of the nineteenth century, in an age when the quantity of publications in the world was still within the bounds of human comprehension, Harvard Librarian John Langdon Sibley thought that "It would be well if it were generally known that there is nothing printed of which the Harvard libraries is not desirous of obtaining a copy."[15]

The development of Harvard's collections owes much to the federated structure of the University; each faculty was responsible for its own library and nearly all chose to build extensive research collections to support the research of their faculties. But it was the influence of one librarian, Archibald Cary Coolidge, who articulated a vision of the comprehensive research library that guided Harvard and perhaps influenced other libraries as well. Not only did Coolidge collect for current faculty needs, but he anticipated future needs by acquiring collections in areas that did not become part of the curriculum or even the research interests of faculty for another fifty years. For example, he gathered materials in the field of Russian, Slavic, and East Asian history and literatures, long before there was active scholarly interest in these parts of the world. No doubt it was Coolidge who Professor Paul Buck had in mind when he said that "possession of a great library, emphasizing new areas of scholarship, enable a university 'to build programs on solid foundations of research materials'."[16]

Coolidge may also have been one of the first librarians to emphasize special collections. He was concerned to collect not just canonical works but all of the literature and documentation that might provide a context for scholarly work. "A collection of single author, no matter how splendid," he said,

> cannot ... be understood without knowledge of his sources, of the influences which surround him and affected him and the results he produced on the minds of others. ... Writings which are neither great nor fashionable stand little chance of being reprinted even when of considerable value. Therefore the originals are all the more necessary for us.[17]

Perhaps such views are indicative of a simpler time when libraries really could aspire to build collections of such breadth and depth. Yet it was an ideal pursued by many libraries and, to a greater degree than we sometimes realize, academic programs developed because of collections.[18] Many public libraries appear to have pursued the same ideal and their research collections are part of the system of resources needed to support research, even if they are frequently ignored by academic research libraries.[19]

The illusion of self-sufficiency seemed to be confirmed by the relative prosperity of libraries in the two decades after World War II. The period between 1950 and 1973 was the longest sustained period of prosperity in history. Wages rose along with productivity while prices fell in relation to buying power; it was the "golden age of industrialism."[20] And the very success of the economy lulled Americans into a false sense of security and the belief that continuing prosperity was somehow inevitable. America was not prepared for the economic challenges that began to occur in the late 1960s. Librarians, like everyone in American society, clung to assumptions—the ideal of self-sufficiency—that began to be undermined by economic reality.

After 1973, increasing book production and the rising cost of publications intersected with declining or at least lower library revenues, a fact well known and often discussed by librarians. Charles Osburn was one of the first to call attention to the disparities between library assumptions about collections—a humanities-based model that called for as comprehensive collections and as complete a record of scholarship (and also the sources needed for scholarship) as possible—and the apparent need for a more focused, patron-centered model that aimed at responsiveness and currency. But, as we have seen, Osburn, Mosher and others were not willing to relieve libraries of their responsibility for acquiring lesser used research materials; rather, they sought cooperative strategies to support the collection of these materials. But the politics of local autonomy and the competitive nature of libraries and, indeed, the universities and institutions of which they are a part, defeated the logic of cooperative collection development.[21] The failures of the Farmington Plan and the National Periodicals Center are indicative of the problems that face cooperative arrangements.

Actually, the idea of self-sufficiency and building encyclopedic collections is not as far fetched as we, in a very different era, are inclined to believe. Traditionally, the literary canon was more or less fixed and authenticating the true text required a fairly limited and certainly definable number of works to understand relations between texts across time. History was dominated by narrative history and centered on great white men and the affairs of nation-states. Historians researched the documentary sources contained in government archives. But the post-World War II expansion of research interests and specializations within academic disciplines was altered, not only by the shifting tides of research, but also by scholars expanding the kinds of documentary sources that might be used in research. Now, literary works, canonical or not, must attend

IMPLICATIONS OF CHANGING INQUIRY
AND EXPANDING RESOURCES ON THE IDEA
OF SELF-SUFFICIENCY

To focus attention on what I believe is the defining issue for research–that is, how to preserve the documentary evidence needed for future research–we must achieve a clearer understanding of how changes in research are challenging library assumptions about building collections and their role in supporting research. There are three aspects to this issue that we need to consider. First, how changes in research affect the requirements for documentary sources. Second, how the expansion of documentary sources affects scholarship. Finally, we must consider how these changes affect the mission of research libraries.

The world of scholarship has been expanding at an astounding rate over the past two generations and the spread of interdisciplinary work into the recesses of nearly every discipline has become the rule, not the exception. Many fields in the humanities and social sciences may be seen as families of disciplines, subdivided by specializations with which they are allied. Literary scholarship, for example, has encouraged interest in materials surrounding literary works such as medical texts, ecclesiastical court records, house wifery manuals, homilies, and other contemporary texts. "The study of religion, once concerned primarily with theology, church history, and biblical studies, has, in recent years, expanded to encompass all world religions and beliefs, embracing 'any aspect of the human encounter with the sacred'."[22] Newer subfields in religious studies draw on the disciplines of anthropology, sociology, psychology, philosophy, history, and literature for both sources and methodology. And nearly every intellectual discipline shows a similar tendency.[23]

History, perhaps more than most disciplines, stands at the intersection between the humanities and social sciences, and historians are often allied with one or more disciplines. Today historians are concerned with a greater variety of human activities than were their predecessors, and their need for documentary sources and data is extremely diffuse. This new history has come to be concerned with virtually every human activity, "total history," in the words of the *Annales* historians. Summarizing these new perspectives, Peter Burke has observed:

> The first half of the century witnessed the rise of the history of ideas. In the last thirty years we have seen a number of remarkable histories of topics which had not previously been thought to possess a history, for example, childhood, death, madness, the climate, smells, dirt and cleanliness, gestures, the body . . . , femininity . . . , reading . . . , speaking, even silence. What had previously been considered as unchanging is now viewed as a 'cultural construction', subject to variation over time as well as in space.[24]

The great problem of the new scholarship and its almost anthropological concern with the world of everyday experience is the problem of evidence and the sources needed for research. But the problem of evidence is a problem of survival and what society values. In a brilliant essay on this topic, Daniel Boorstin describes the ephemeral nature of evidence under such descriptive headings as: "The Bias of Survival," "Law of the Survival of the Unread," "Survival of the Academically Classifiable," and "Survival of Objects Which Are Not Used or Which Have High Intrinsic Value." His point is that stately mansions survive, but transportable houses of the poor do not; learned treatises on Puritan theology survive, often in mint condition, but scarcely an example of the more than three million copies of the *New England Primer* can be found today.[25] Future inquiry, then, depends on the evidence that survives. The question is, who is responsible for preserving it?

A second issue is the way in which the discoveries and use of new documentary sources change research. Expanding research horizons and the proliferation of specialized fields within various academic disciplines create an interplay between scholarly interests and documentary sources that was less apparent in the past when the focus of most academic disciplines was more certain. Now, however, documentary sources themselves–those which are consid-

THE FUTURE OF RESOURCE SHARING

ered authoritative, as well as new ones—are part of the intellectual argument about academic disciplines and new directions in research.

For example, Philippe Aries redefined the domain of documentary evidence by using school registers and illustrations in late medieval hour books to explore the nature of the family in pre-modern society. In a later study, he used sculpture, tombstones, wills and testaments, letters, paintings, diaries and sanitation reports to document a study of death.[26] Fernand Braudel's famous 1949 study, *The Mediterranean,* attracted attention because of the amount of space he devoted to the physical environment. Today, one cannot consider the great historic migrations or demographic changes in history without considering the scientific evidence about volcanic eruptions and other dramatic changes in prehistoric climate.[27]

One consequence of introducing new research sources has been the redefinition of academic disciplines. For example, the French analiste, Marc Bloch, convinced that agrarian history could no longer be discussed only in legal and institutional terms, redefined agricultural history by using documentary evidence previously ignored by historians.[28] Bloch used old maps, the etymology and distribution of place names, the design of premodern agricultural tools and even aerial surveys. These were not new sources, but in recognizing the relevance of sources historians had not used before, Bloch changed the discipline and the kinds of questions scholars would henceforth ask.[29]

Something of the same effect is occurring because of the sudden opening of sources previously closed to scholars. The collapse of the former Soviet Union and Eastern Europe is a case in point; the gradual lifting of the veil in Chinese libraries and archives is another. At a recent conference concerning the opening of China's archives, several historians commented on the way in which access to archives had altered our understanding of China and its peoples and culture. "It is striking to recall," said Professor William Kirby, "that the major works that defined the field in the West until recent years were based on little or no Chinese archival evidence. The opening of China's archives," says Kirby, "will begin to close this archival gap as old fields are revisited and new ones initiated."[30]

New technology also changes and expands our definition of documentation and affects research and the range of sources that are potentially useful for research. Digital information is malleable, the author uncertain, and the authority of the "text" is clearly diminished.[31] Moreover, in a digital universe, the arts–texts, sounds, images–share a common base and may in fact become interchangeable. As Richard Lanham has observed, "the separation of the arts does not inhere in nature; they have always drawn as close together as they could. It is the expressive medium which has kept them apart."[32]

Aside from its overwhelming presence in our lives, part of our fascination with information technology is its potential to transform scholarly communication and even our definition of what constitutes the "record of scholarship" and ultimately the Library itself. Electronic communication, like the critique of the rules of evidence by feminists, blacks, and ethnic groups, challenges the "sites of control over the organization, production, 'quality control' and distribution of knowledge."[33] The question is, how do we "document" the creative process that designs buildings using CAD? Or, to take a more traditional tack, how do we authenticate a text written with a word processor? Is it possible to ask the same questions about the product and creative process that employ different technologies? Should university libraries content themselves with preserving and providing access to the record of scholarship or should they take literally Archibald Carey Coolidge's admonition that no author can "be understood without knowledge of his sources, of the influences which surround him and affected him and the results he produced on the minds of others?" In the emerging electronic world, where information is generally licensed and the processes for using it are subject to patents, how can critical information be preserved and who will do it?[34] What, then, is the role of the library in supporting research in such a diverse research environment?

IMPLICATIONS OF CHANGING RESEARCH AND SOURCES FOR LIBRARIES

Changes in research and the growing demand for new sources have had three important implications for libraries. First, the idea of the self-sufficient research library has been exposed. Second, some library practices and assumptions are being altered. Third, the competitive model of support for research within higher education is being undermined. Finally, the implications of these changes for libraries suggest the need for a national system of research in which sharing resources will be a critical ingredient for success.

We may agree that scholars today are more multidisciplinary in their research and also recognize that broader research horizons promote interest in a variety of new documentary sources. What has been most neglected, however, is a discussion of the implications of these changes for research libraries. One reason for this neglect is that our thinking about the purpose of libraries has been shaped by academic disciplines based on the technology of print. That is, we tend not to see and understand that scholarship, and the libraries that support it, are also an invention, a technology of scholarship, subject to historical interpretation, like any other social institution. In short, research institutions, including libraries, are inevitably affected by the redefinition of disciplines and a need for different kinds of documentation. What, then, are the implications of such change for research libraries and how will it alter them? And what are the implications of such an altered landscape for resource sharing?

Research has become transinstitutional, and the patterns of research and the need for a variety of new sources undermine the possibility of a comprehensive research library as the principal support for academic research. Library collection policies have generally served the definitions of knowledge of traditional academic disciplines; that is, the Library supports the disciplinary definition of a field of knowledge and attempts to objectively select books according to the principles of the discipline. But if the authority of the disciplines and the documentary evidence needed to support them is challenged, a traditional strength of the research library is undermined.

Another implication of the new patterns of research and scholarship is that academic departments no longer necessarily reflect the research interests of their members. Research is increasingly interdisciplinary;[35] individual scholars are linked across departments into small interinstitutional communities of scholars, drawn to one another by shared research interests to form an invisible college that is not reflected in the formal structure of the university. The continuing fragmentation of knowledge will create new "communities" whose research interests are likely to go beyond local resources and transcend the library's ability to respond effectively and in a timely fashion. This tension between changing research interests and traditional library practice is evident in the cataloging and classification of books, which reflect traditional academic disciplines, and do not provide the kind of access most desirable for the newer forms of research.[36]

The enormous expansion of potential sources needed for research, even more than limited funding, exposes the myth of self-sufficiency and the encyclopedic library. The number and variety of sources desired for research also exposes the bibliocentricism of library practice. When nonprint or nonbook sources were relatively few and seen as essentially ancillary to research in published sources, there was an understandable tendency to define library practice, especially cataloging, in terms of published sources. But with the increasing emphasis on contextual information and nonprint sources, the limits of this view were exposed. The incorporation of records of nonbook formats into national utilities and local catalogs is evidence of this change; the adoption of format integration in US MARC confirms it. What is emerging from these changes is a cultural database that points to research sources regardless of their format, genre, or location.

Changes in research and the broader inquiry of multidisciplinary research extends the scope of research collections beyond the record of scholarship.[37] While not abandoning traditional print sources, libraries will be under pressure to be more aggressive in collecting material generally called "special collections." A conference on Research Trends and Library Resources revealed a remarkable consensus among a group of scholars drawn from a cross section of the humanities and social sciences "that libraries needed to acquire not only the traditional published sources but also 'nontraditional' research materials—images, including photographs and motion picture film, popular literature, even advertising and other forms of ephemera, spatial data, personal papers and archives, artifacts, raw economic and social data, and virtually anything else that might reflect the attitudes, activities, and culture of society."[38] The

THE FUTURE OF RESOURCE SHARING

list is as long as one cares to make it and has the resources with which to support it. As one scholar put it, just as the boundaries between academic disciplines are weakening, so too may the boundaries between libraries, archives, museums, and historical societies. In truth, the sources for research have always extended beyond those of any one library, but these scholars, perhaps because they saw their own research gravitating to multiple cultural sources, thought that the concept of the research library ought to be reinvented.

One implication of such a change will be the convergence of library principles and archival theory and practice. Archives are not discipline or even subject based; they are meta-disciplinary and meta-documentary and are not bound to one form of documentation or the research agenda of any particular discipline. As libraries begin to collect the variety of evidence needed for research, they will need to pay attention not only to the evidence and fact but also the context in which evidence is embedded. And looking beyond discrete facts to the context in which they appear is precisely what much of the new multidisciplinary research is about. This is a very different perspective from traditional library principles and will have substantial implications for how libraries provide intellectual access to documentary sources. For example, by expanding the definition of documentary evidence and taking a meta-disciplinary approach to documentation, we encounter and perhaps offend the rules of cataloging that have been developed out of the tradition of printing and the idea of permanence which it entails. Researchers navigating a rich mix of primary and secondary sources need scanning knowledge of sources, regardless of their form or genre. In this transinstitutional environment, research libraries will become the hubs of an information distribution network providing access to electronic databases, in which the library's catalog is only one among many databases, only some of which reside in the library. This is a very different idea from the traditional library catalog, which provides access to the library's own holdings. But in the new model the library and its catalog no longer occupy a privileged position; what you have is information about sources and, ultimately, the sources themselves.

If research is becoming transinstitutional, support for research still depends on autonomous institutions. Higher education in America is based on a competitive model in which universities, even public ones, are essentially autonomous and compete with one another for students, faculty, and financial resources. An important element in this competition is research which, perhaps more than anything else, is the measure of success in this competition. Support for research through laboratories and libraries is therefore an essential ingredient in the competitive academic model. Competition among libraries for prize collections or the largest number of volumes is simply an extension of this model and is intrinsic to American higher education.[39]

These changes are undermining the original purpose of research libraries. No one institution can support the demands being made by changing research. Efforts to create a two-tiered collaborative system for supporting lesser-used materials have thus far failed to produce the national system for research that is clearly needed to preserve our cultural heritage and support research. We have made significant progress in building an infrastructure for sharing resources; what we also need is a system for cooperative collection development and a national agency to guide and direct the efforts of independent resource centers dedicated to supporting research.

RESOURCE SHARING IN A TRANSINSTITUTIONAL ENVIRONMENT

There are two challenges for resource sharing. First, how can we restore collaborative collection development as an integral part of resource sharing and create a national system of research that honors scholars as well as the sources needed for research? Second, how can we create an institutional and organizational structure that includes the enormous number and variety of associations, both academic and professional, and create a forum for making the decisions that must increasingly be made at a national level? To support research in a transinstitutional environment we must develop a national framework to guide autonomous cultural institutions and provide a way to marshall and direct financial resources, both public and private, to preserve our cultural heritage. These are complex issues and I can only suggest one or two ideas for consideration here. But I believe that the rising interest in resource sharing sug-

20 *THE FUTURE OF RESOURCE SHARING*

gests that the time has come to explore these and other proposals; improved bibliographic access and delivery of information can provide the means to make it work.

The need for a national system of research resources has long been recognized by librarians; it was the underlying assumption of the Farmington Plan, the Conspectus and various other proposals for cooperative collection development. Moreover, recent proposals, such as the call for an electronic library by Brian Hawkins[40] and now the Library of Congress,[41] are important attempts to think about library sources as a national research system that can correct the limitations of individual libraries. Transinstitutional research requires a national or even an international system of resources to support it. Currently, the system of research sources exists as the aggregation of collections held by research libraries, historical societies, archives museums, and electronic information, both networked and local. In fact, it can be defined as the aggregation of all information and materials, regardless of form or genre, that can be used for research. The problem is how to encourage autonomous institutions to collect materials for a discipline or a national system at a time when most libraries are cutting back.

DEVELOPING COLLECTIONS: AN INTEGRATED REGIONAL MODEL

One model to consider for collaborative collection development is based on the Integrated Regional Model that has been proposed by environmental researchers. The idea of an integrated model can take at least two forms: an integrated regional model or an integrated cultural model. The regional model is the one that has been followed by a coalition of environmental scientists and social scientists. The inspiration for the integrated regional model is ecology, a discipline that arose out of the integration of older, established fields of study. Obviously, the idea of a region, as a distinct physical entity within a continent or world environment, puts parameters around a very complex conceptual and informational environment.[42] A variation on this idea is a cultural model that integrates scholars and resources needed to study problems concerning a particular ethnic group, a country, or a subject. To document a particular intellectual domain we will need evidence that reveals interactions and relationships among people, organizations, and ideas–a kind of seamless web of interconnections–that is neither restricted to nor defined by current academic disciplines.

Researching any intellectual domain requires a system of evidence and sources that include all forms of evidence, regardless of form or genre, and all institutions that have responsibility for preserving it. We need to get away from conceptual distinctions among libraries, archives, museums, historical societies. Instead, we must think of them as part of a system of sources needed to document a research domain. Moreover, people, as well as sources, are part of a system of research, that is, both the users and providers of research sources are part of an integrated model of research. By focusing on the interests and affinities of a particular community or intellectual domain instead of the interests and obligations of an entire university or research library, there may be a better chance for successful collaboration. One of the reasons previous collaborative efforts have not fared well is because research libraries are obliged to support the research interests of a diverse academic population and the very diversity of interests within the community tends to undermine broad-based collaboration. However, by focusing on an area of affinity, a particular intellectual or cultural domain, there may be a better chance to build the kind of partnerships among institutions with related interests that would permit them to divide responsibility for preserving the documentary sources their community will need. In a sense, one would collect for the system or domain, that is, the community of scholars interested in a particular domain. Better bibliographic access and improved delivery for sharing these resources will also increase our prospects for success.

There are several reasons to consider the idea of the Integrated Regional Model as a way of orchestrating collaborative collection development. First, by focusing on broadly defined research domains–for example, the environment, gender or ethnic groups–we more nearly mirror the reality of transinstitutional research, rather than the academic disciplines that arose in the nineteenth century. Because these are newer areas of research and therefore less wedded to traditional library structures, faculty are more likely to be receptive to the idea of shared resources. Indeed, like the scholars who participated in the Conference on Research Trends cited earlier, they will recognize the necessity of doing so. Second, because the initiative or at least support for shared resources comes from the faculty and others who have an interest in a particular intellectual domain, there is likely to be less resistance to cooperative collection development within the institution. Third, by partializing the problem, that is, by focusing on a part of the community and its research resources, one creates a more manageable task than if one tries to build a coalition across an entire institution. Fourth, orientation toward an integrated model of resources shared by many institutions becomes a more attractive target for funding agencies. Cooperative projects to provide access to information or to digitize and preserve materials are more likely to be funded than if the proposal comes from a single institution, thus providing an additional incentive for collaboration. Finally, a truly integrated system of research must be seen as a kind of cultural reservoir, in which reciprocity is a principal component. Viewed as a system, any institution, even the smallest, can make a contribution to and participate in an integrated model of research resources.

A NATIONAL SYSTEM FOR RESEARCH

Although individual institutions may collaborate to develop collections, thereby restoring a missing ingredient in resource sharing, we must also develop a national organization or institution for supporting it. There are two issues we need to consider. First, many of the issues concerning research, especially in the emerging electronic world, are national issues that can no longer be addressed locally. Second, if, as I have argued, research is beyond the capacity of universities to support, then we must reconsider the purpose of research, who benefits from it, and how it can be supported.

One aspect of the emerging transinstitutional environment is the decrease in local autonomy over some issues that are important for research. Information technology is undermining local decision-making by research libraries and universities and will ultimately require a very different structure for supporting academic research. Decisions, which in the past were regarded as within the purview of a university or library, will increasingly be made at a national level. Questions concerning copyright, what constitutes a publication or fair use of networked information, generic software developments that benefit academic research, the use of patents for system-level processes, the growing need for standards for electronic information, all require a national forum. The underlying rationale for university and library support for research is thus being undermined by forces that are beyond the control of individual institutions; neither libraries nor universities can decide independently how to resolve these matters.

To effectively address these issues we need an organization or perhaps several organizations that would bring together scholars (the consumers of research sources) and the various groups responsible for preserving information (the providers of research sources) and bring these perspectives to bear on issues affecting the national system of research and its sources. To be successful, we will need extraordinary leadership to change the venue of academic research from the exclusive purview of the campus to a national concern and, second, to persuade the nation of the value of research as a common good. Creating an institutional framework for a national agenda for research will not be easy because it runs counter to the competitive and voluntaristic ethos of the country; persuading the country that research is a common good that ought to be publicly supported will also not be easy in an era that profoundly distrusts government and most national institutions.

The public has begun to question the value of academic research and to see it as an entitlement of a privileged class. But if we believe research is a public good, then should it not be supported by the public for the good of all? In the end, we must acknowledge that voluntarism is not enough and that a national system of research requires national support for the resources required for research. Perhaps a model to consider is the agricultural extension program that directly relates research to a constituency that experiences its benefits. Yet another model, perhaps more appropriate for the humanities and social sciences, is a Canadian model in which national institutions, for example, the National Archives of Canada, are responsible not only for the preservation of the nation's cultural heritage, but also for assisting and supporting those professions concerned with these activities.[43] It is precisely the absence of a national forum in this country, an agency, public or private, that

24 THE FUTURE OF RESOURCE SHARING

effectively knits together the various associations and professional groups concerned with preserving our intellectual heritage, that is the principal obstacle in creating a national system of research.

CONCLUSION

Information technology offers an opportunity to create the national system of resources we will need to support research in the future. The first fruits of this revolution can be seen in the expanded access to catalogs of primary and secondary sources and enormous improvements in the delivery of information. Burgeoning interest in and development of the mechanics of resource sharing are indicative of these changes. But technology cannot alone ensure the preservation of collections and primary sources required for research in a transinstitutional age. Not only do we need to restore the primacy of collections in our conception of resource sharing, but we must devise new organizational models and institutional structures to preserve the information that is essential for research.

NOTES

1. George Gilder, *Life After Television: The Coming Transformation of Media and American Life* (Knoxville, TN: Whittle Direct Books, 1990), 25.

2. See Richard De Gennaro, *Library Support: The Invisible Crisis, Report of the Director of Libraries, University of Pennsylvania, 1980-81* (Philadelphia, PA: University of Pennsylvania Libraries, 1981).

3. Kendon Stubbs, quoted in *ARL: A Bimonthly Newsletter of Research Library Issues and Actions* (May 1994):1-2.

4. *ARL*, 2.

5. "Creating the Library of the Future: Incrementalism Won't Get Us There!" photocopy of manuscript. Hawkins argues, correctly I think, that the problem is structural and will require a new model or paradigm that goes well beyond the ability of individual institutions to fix.

6. Charles B. Osburn, *Academic Research and Library Resources: Changing Patterns in America* (Westport, CT: Greenwood Press, 1979), 140.

7. "The Research Library and Emerging Information Technology," *New Directions for Teaching and Learning* 51 (Fall): 86.

8. Vicki Anders, Collen Cook, and Roberta Pitts, "A Glimpse into a Crystal Ball: Academic Libraries in the Year 2000," *Wilson Library Bulletin* 67 (October 1992): 37.

9. *ARL*.

10. Joseph J. Branin, "Delivering on Promises: the Intersection of Print and Electronic Information Systems in Libraries," *Information Technology and Libraries* 10 (December 1992): 327.

11. Karen Horny, "New Turns for A New Century: Library Services in the Information Era," *Library Resources and Technical Services* 31 (January/March 1987): 6-11.

12. Hannah King, "Walls Around the Electronic Library," *The Electronic Library* 11 (June, 1993): 165-74.

13. Joseph J. Branin, "Cooperative Collection Development," in *Collection Management: A New Treatise*, ed. Charles B. Osburn and Ross Atkinson (Greenwich, CT: JAI Press Inc., 1991), 95-101.

14. Gerald Greenberg and Alain Giffard, "New Orders of Knowledge, New Technologies of Reading," *Representations* (Spring 1993): 80.

15. Quoted in a paper presented by Kenneth Carpenter at the Heritage of the Graphic Arts Lecture series (New York City 1981).

16. Quoted in William Bentinck-Smith, *Building A Great Library: The Coolidge Years at Harvard* (Cambridge, MA: Harvard University Press, 1976), 4-5.

17. Quoted in *Building a Great Library*, 140.

18. For a charming illustration of how this happens in universities like Harvard, see "Pointing Our Thoughts," an address by President Neil L. Rudenstine on the occasion of the launch of The University Campaign, May 14, 1994.

19. Marilyn Gell Mason, "Is There a Global Role for Metropolitan City Libraries?" *American Libraries* 25 (September 1994): 734-38.

20. Paul Hawken, *The Next Economy* (New York: Holt, Rinehart and Winston, 1983), 22-23.

21. Branin, "Cooperative Collection Development," 105.

22. Constance C. Gould has compiled a very useful survey of the information needs of scholars in the sciences, humanities, and social sciences in three volumes, prepared for the Program for Research Information Management of the Research Libraries Group. This quote is from *Information Needs in the Humanities: An Assessment* (Stanford, CA: Research Libraries Group, 1988), 34.

23. Greenberg and Giffard, "New Orders of Knowledge," 83.

24. Peter Burke, "Overture: The New History, its Past and its Future," in *New Perspectives on Historical Writing*, ed. Peter Burke (University Park, PA: The Pennsylvania State University Press, 1991), 3.

25. Daniel J. Boorstin, "A Wrestler With the Angel," *Hidden History* (New York, NY: Harper and Row, 1987), 3-23.

26. Constance C. Gould, "2020 Visions: Trends in Research," *The American Archivist* 57 (Winter 1994): 133.

27. A good summary of the way scientific evidence is affecting historical understanding can be seen in chapter 3, "Climate and Civilization: A Short History," in Albert Gore's *Earth in the Balance: Ecology and the Human Spirit* (New York, NY: Plume, 1993).

28. Marc Bloch, *French Rural History: An Essay on its Basic Characteristics*. Trans. Janet Sondheimer (London: Routledge & Kegan Paul, 1978), xiii-xiv.

26   THE FUTURE OF RESOURCE SHARING

29. Gould, "2020 Visions," 133.

30. William Kirby, "Notes on the Opening of Archives and Western Scholarship on Republican History," paper presented at the Conference on Modern Chinese Historical Archives, University of California at Berkeley (August 1994).

31. Jay David Bolter, *Writing Space: The Computer, Hypertext, and the History of Writing* (Hillsdale, NJ: Erlbaum, 1991), 2.

32. "A Computer-based *Harvard Red Book*: General Education in the Digital Age," paper delivered at the conference, "Gateways to Knowledge: the Changing Role of Academic Libraries in Learning, Teaching, and Research." Harvard University, 5-6 November 1993.

33. Peter Lyman, "Invention, the Mother of Necessity: Archival Research in 2020," *American Archivist* 57 (Winter 1994): 123.

34. I have said little about the problem of preserving the historical record in an electronic age. It is, however, a very important issue that has enormous implications for the preservation of our cultural heritage. For a sobering perspective on the problems posed by electronic information, see Clifford A. Lynch, "Rethinking the Integrity of the Scholarly Record in the Networked Information Age," *Educom Review* 29 (March/April, 1994): 38-40.

35. The common notion that research has become interdisciplinary or, more accurately, multidisciplinary, was empirically demonstrated by Paul Metz, *The Landscape of Literatures: Use of Subject Collections in a University Library* (Chicago: American Library Association, 1983), 88-94.

36. Karen Markey and Diane Visne-Goetz, "Increasing the Accessibility of Library of Congress Subject Headings in Online Bibliographic Systems," *Annual Review of OCLC Research, 1987-88* (1988), 32-34.

37. Eldred Smith maintains that library's primary obligation is to collect "the accumulating record of scholarship." *The Librarian, the Scholar, and the Future of the Research Library* (Westport, CT: Greenwood Press, 1990), 2.

38. Lawrence Dowler, "Conference on Research Trends and Library Resources," *Harvard Library Bulletin* 1 (Summer 1990), 5-6.

39. I have tried to describe the challenges to the traditional system in greater detail in "The Implications of Electronic Information for National Institutions," *Leonardo* 27 (1994): 171-78.

40. Brian L. Hawkins, "Planning for the National Electronic Library," *Educom Review: Learning, Communications and Information Technology* 29 (May/June 1994): 19-29.

41. "Library of Congress Offering to Feed Data Superhighway," *New York Times* (September 15, 1994), A10.

42. "Integrated Regional Models: Analysis of Interactions Between Humans and Their Environment," Report to the National Science Foundation on a Workshop held at the Institute of Ecosystem Studies, Millbrook, New York, 4-8 October 1992 (December 1992).

43. For a description of this idea that was accepted and implemented in Canada, see Terry Eastwood, "Attempts at National Planning for Archives in Canada, 1975-1985," *The Public Historian* 8 (Summer 1986): 74-91.

Resource Sharing:
The Public University Library's
Imperative

Nancy L. Eaton

PUBLIC UNIVERSITIES AND THE PUBLIC GOOD

By virtue of their tax-exempt status, receipt of public funding from state appropriations, and their tripartite roles of teaching, research, and service, public universities have an implied contract to serve the public good. According to the Morrill Act of 1862, land grant universities have a special responsibility for educating the "industrial classes in the several pursuits and professions of life" and in technology transfer, originally focused on agriculture and the mechanical arts but now more broadly interpreted. Accordingly, citizens of each state have an expectation that their public universities serve a role beyond their primary clientele of faculty, students, and staff. As part of the university, libraries are held to the same standard for serving the public good. Because tax funds help support libraries, citizens expect research libraries in public universities to be available to them and to serve the larger goals of information delivery in the state.

This was an understandable expectation when state legislatures funded their universities appropriate to this level of service. How-

---

Nancy L. Eaton is Dean of Library Services at Iowa State University in Ames, IA.

[Haworth co-indexing entry note]: "Resource Sharing: The Public University Library's Imperative." Eaton, Nancy L. Co-published simultaneously in *Journal of Library Administration* (The Haworth Press, Inc.) Vol. 21, No. 1/2, 1995, pp. 27-38; and *The Future of Resource Sharing* (ed: Shirley K. Baker, and Mary E. Jackson) The Haworth Press, Inc., 1995, pp. 27-38. Multiple copies of this article/chapter may be purchased from The Haworth Document Delivery Center [1-800-342-9678; 9:00 a.m. - 5:00 p.m. (EST)].

© 1995 by The Haworth Press, Inc. All rights reserved.

THE FUTURE OF RESOURCE SHARING

ever, in the last several decades, that tax support has slipped dramatically. Public universities previously described as "publicly supported" are now frequently described as "publicly affiliated" because of the reduced funding provided by state legislatures. For example, the University of Vermont receives only 13 percent of its total budget from the Vermont legislature; and currently Iowa State University receives 31 percent from the Iowa legislature. Figures of 30-35 percent are commonly reported in the press. As state funding has declined, universities have had to look elsewhere for that support from sources such as research overhead, federal grants, foundation and corporation grants, private giving, and fees. Libraries are in the position of receiving funding from sources that cannot be rationalized to provide service to secondary users and are even encouraged to generate sources of revenue by charging fees for service.

At the same time that support for serving the public is going down, definitions of service are changing and expectations going up. This phenomenon is commented on in several papers prepared for Iowa State University's current strategic planning process begun in 1993, which is to culminate in a new strategic plan for 1995-2000. Steffen Schmidt, professor of political science, points out:

> Another policy initiative that speaks to cost and funding is 'national service' and 'community service'. This promises to be one of the new federal policies which determines a growing portion of student scholarship funding. We can also expect state government to pick up on this model. Thus the university should be prepared to offer initiatives in this area and in apprenticeship, funded internship, and co-op programs. Moreover, leaner ways of delivering education through distance learning and through the coming 'electronic superhighway' will also be required. Moreover, there is growing pressure for research universities to form consortia with each other, with colleges, and to enter into cost sharing arrangements with private industry.[1]

Similar observations are made by faculty reviewing the changing university roles in continuing education, distance education, and technology transfer:

Outreach, the third of the three components of the University's mission, is defined as the extension of services to accommodate those who cannot come to the university. Outreach is considered the service aspect of the university and is designed to satisfy the needs of the public. Many within the continuing education profession consider the borders of the state to be the appropriate extension of the land grant university's campus. Increasingly, continuing education is seen as a national and even an international activity of the land grant university. Outreach is multifaceted, and one portion of the outreach function is EXTENDED AND CONTINUING EDUCATION . . . Library and media resources should be available to students electronically whenever possible. If hard-copy versions of library and media resources are needed there should be an electronic ordering system available for students who are off-campus.[2]

External factors have increasingly motivated universities to partner. Governments and industry have pressured universities to contribute more directly to reversing the decline in the U.S. competitiveness position. This has stimulated the formation of university partnerships with industry. Funding cuts for research at universities due to federal and state budget reductions have forced universities to seek funding from industry, consortia, and other sources through partnerships. The federal labs have followed suit.[3]

These observations about the changing expectations for public institutions also forecast changing expectations for research libraries in public universities. No longer can the library administration and staff define its primary clientele as on-campus faculty, students, and staff, with minimal support for off-campus university employees such as extension staff. Due to new expectations for distance learning and continuing education, the campus is the state, and students can be geographically located anywhere within the state boundaries. The university's service mission now includes technology transfer from university research into product development; and the state has expectations for help with economic development to expand the tax base and to create new jobs for its citizens. The

30   THE FUTURE OF RESOURCE SHARING

university library is thus called upon to provide service to research parks and state industry as information becomes an ever more important component of economic development and technology transfer. And it is expected to coordinate with the state library and other public, academic, school, and special libraries within the state and nation to provide information needed by the general citizen.

CATCH 22 FOR LIBRARIES: DEMAND vs. FUNDING

At the same time that expectations for library services are rising, funding for research libraries is declining. Kendon Stubbs summarizes this trend in the introduction to the annual statistics gathered by the Association of Research Libraries (ARL) for 1992/93. This data shows that the 1993 expenditures are nearly twice as much as libraries spent for serials in 1986 but purchased 5 percent fewer subscriptions than the libraries maintained in 1986. To help pay for rising serial prices, monograph expenditures dropped by 10 percent during this same period, resulting in 23 percent fewer monograph titles purchased in 1993 as in 1986. Equally distressing, since 1986 the student population has increased by 11 percent while the median ARL library had the same number of total staff in 1993 as in 1986; and many actually lost staff during the budget cuts of the early 1990s. The only statistics to have gone up significantly between 1986 and 1993 are those for interlibrary lending (41 percent) and interlibrary borrowing (77 percent), a reflection of an expanding universe of information, a smaller locally owned percentage of that universe, and resultant interlibrary borrowing even for undergraduates.[4] The declining percentage of the university's budget that goes to support of the university library is documented in the Mellon Foundation study of university libraries.[5] Thus, university libraries are being asked to provide services and make collections available to an expanding on-campus and off-campus student body and to citizens of the state with information needs, as well as to increase services to support new expectations for extension, technology transfer, distance learning and continuing education.

In addition to these new programmatic expectations, research librarians, as part of the larger library community, add their own expectations based upon their professional service mission. Librarians believe strongly in public access to information, including government information created at taxpayer expense, as a foundation for citizens to participate in a democratic society and as a fundamental principle of intellectual freedom. As part of the infrastructure for scholarly communication which presupposes free exchange of ideas in the scholarly community, necessary for the creation of new knowledge, libraries also have a long history of sharing resources with scholars from other universities through interlibrary loan.

IMPLICATIONS FOR THE FUTURE OF RESOURCE SHARING

The challenge for the public university research library in the 1990s is to find ways of funding the rising expectations for service while preserving their contribution to the "public good," to intellectual freedom, and to scholarly communication to support the creation of new knowledge, in an era of declining financial support. There is no indication that the financial picture will reverse itself, given the economic pressures facing higher education in general. As a result, technology is held out as one solution to this dilemma. A variety of publications document the promise of computing and information technology as they might control costs and provide new capabilities not even imagined.[6] Another common theme is that information is now a commodity, and that users should be expected to pay for information in recognition of its value; that information now is a critical component of the U.S. economy and of U.S. competitiveness. This does not take into account any of the above issues regarding the public good, intellectual freedom, or free flow of scholarly information. Nor does it provide for archiving of information that has marginal or no apparent commercial value of the moment.

Research libraries have a responsibility in this environment to facilitate resource sharing and archiving of scholarly information for purposes that supersede economic value; and publicly affiliated research libraries have a particular responsibility of protecting the public's interests. Some strategies are already being employed by libraries; and a host of questions being raised also suggest new avenues for investigation. There are differing opinions among research library directors, however, on how best to proceed or how to finance these efforts. Therefore, these issues are being pursued very much on an ad hoc, local option basis.

Consortia. Libraries, like universities, have resorted to consortia of various sorts to pool their resources. The Research Libraries Group (RLG) was formed to focus on resource sharing among research libraries. The Online Computer Library Center, Inc. (OCLC) has as its major objectives helping libraries reduce the rate of rise of costs, and further access to the world's information. Both of these organizations were formed by libraries in the early 1970s as not-for-profit membership consortia. Each has had a profound effect on research libraries' ability to expand resource sharing by use of technology. Of recent note is the subscription pricing and block pricing offered by OCLC to libraries for electronic information which, in effect, provides lower prices based upon bulk purchase from publishers by guaranteeing a certain level of use by member libraries.

The Center for Research Libraries (CRL) is a consortium that accepts little-used research materials and holds them in its facilities in Chicago for use by any of its members, thus reducing the number of copies stored nationally, thereby reducing space requirements for member libraries. It also collects in specialized areas, thus eliminating the need for other research libraries to do so. Member libraries pay an annual fee to support the operating costs for the Center, and non-members pay for use of the material.

The Coalition for Networked Information (CNI) has concentrated on development of technical infrastructure and technical standards that would facilitate use of electronic information as an alternative to print and microforms. Regional and state library consortia also pool their resources to contain costs and maximize access for their constituencies.

Centers of excellence. If Brian Hawkins is correct in his projections of inflation in the publishing industry, "by the year 2026, the acquisitions budgets of our finest libraries will have only 20 percent of the buying power they had forty-five years earlier."[7] This trend has focused attention on identifying certain research libraries as "centers of excellence" for specific materials, whether by subject coverage, language, country of origin, or other definitions of coverage. Libraries could reallocate funds away from areas in which they would accept less comprehensive holdings in order to fund acquisitions in their "centers of excellence." They would rely on other libraries for lesser used materials in areas which were not their specialties. This approach would guarantee that certain libraries within the U.S. would be collecting comprehensively within defined areas or subjects for the public good.

This approach does not answer the question of how to fund access to external users requiring services from these "centers of excellence," since these collections would be serving a national and even international clientele. Costs for making the materials widely available would be determined by the mission of the library and definitions of its primary versus secondary constituencies. A case can be made, however, that secondary constituencies should pay for access or document delivery, since acquisitions and access costs for these materials will far exceed the capability of the library or university to fund them on behalf of a national or international constituency. An alternative approach would be to incorporate these centers into existing consortia such as the Center for Research Libraries, whereby consortia members would have access and contribute to their acquisitions costs; and non-members would pay higher per request charges. Supplemental federal funding would be logical, given the national role that these centers would have; but this is unlikely, given the current federal debt.

Definition of core services. Universities and libraries have defined certain services that will be paid for by the institution as a universal service to its public. For instance, Internet membership charges are paid by the computing center as a core service provided to faculty, students, and staff; and the services provided by the network are perceived by users to be free. Likewise, most library services and access to library collections traditionally have been perceived as centrally provided services free to individual users. Fees for specialized services have been added in a helter-skelter manner as each library added new services and decided whether or not to add charges to cover those services. An example is charging for librarian-facilitated (mediated) online searching which was viewed initially by librarians as a "value-added service" when print versions of the same information were also available to patrons; it is more difficult to rationalize this service as "value-added" now that libraries are cancelling print versions to save money or as information is available only in an electronic format. Assuming an end-user search capability exists in addition to librarian-facilitated searching, however, it still could be viewed as "value-added," since patrons would still have the option of doing the work themselves. Likewise, some libraries differentiate between an interlibrary loan transaction that is traditionally sent or received by mail versus a faxed copy, again assuming that choices exist and that extra labor or costs are involved. As the methods for requesting or sending materials becomes more the determination of the library rather than the patron, in order to reduce costs, labor, or time, the patron has fewer choices; under those circumstances, should the patron be charged? Increasingly, libraries are stressing patron-initiated online services in order to minimize labor costs to the library and to thereby minimize costs passed on to the patron.

One approach to this dilemma is for librarians to define a core set of services available to a library's primary clientele without charge, based upon today's models and technology for acquiring, storing, and disseminating information. This conceptualization of core services is best done collectively as a profession if we are to convey a systematic message to our local clientele. The definitions may be different depending upon whether the library's parent institution is public or private.

Definition of value-added services. Assuming that librarians and other information professionals can agree on a definition or definitions of core services, then a similar common schema for "value-added" services, with appropriate charges for services rendered, might be constructed. Again, conceptualization of "value-added" services is best done collectively if we are to convey a systematic message to our local clientele. This approach would also address the expectation by an increasing number of universities that libraries will generate new sources of income; it would help clarify when this is feasible and under what conditions.

Reallocation of resources. Once core services were defined and agreed upon between the library administration and the university administration, some reallocation of university and library funds could take place to protect those core services. Cost recovery for value-added services would be used to support those services directly on a demand basis. While some reallocation might be needed, the ability to present a coherent definition of core and value-added services to primary and secondary patrons would be a major step forward.

Redefinition of primary clientele and consortial partnerships. As indicated earlier, land grant universities in particular and public universities more generally are experiencing rising expectations regarding their responsibilities to the state and its citizens, resulting in a broader definition of primary clientele. Libraries are expected to support library and information needs of students geographically dispersed throughout the state and to support needs of citizens, state agencies, and private corporations in technology transfer and economic development. Publishers have not recognized these changing definitions of primary and secondary clientele. Licensing agreements for database access still tend to define access based upon a definition of campus users; and myriad obstacles exist for remote access to electronic reserve collections or document delivery to off-site patrons. The application of "fair use" under current copyright law needs to be applied to electronic versions of publications for use by a decentralized client base. Likewise, licensing agreements ignore the need for recognition of specially defined but legitimate clientele at distance learning sites or part of consortial memberships. Where these have been recognized, they have been individually negotiated and are not subject to general knowledge within the profession. This need has been hindered by lack of the ability within our computer systems to track users by institution or to provide sophisticated security validation in order to guarantee the license provider that the library or computer center is honoring the intent of the license. Software is beginning to incorporate those necessary capabilities.

Information technology and distributed computing. Client-server architecture and new telecommunications technology (e.g., fiber optic and slip technology) finally are making distributed computing and distribution of electronic information to the desktop workstation realizable goals. Universities and libraries must still make significant capital investments in the systems and services that will utilize these technologies to reduce the costs of information storage and dissemination and to provide new platforms for library and

36   *THE FUTURE OF RESOURCE SHARING*

information services. Research libraries are in the midst of a "sea change" with regard to how they can use these technologies effectively on behalf of their patrons and on behalf of the public good. It is incumbent upon them to keep their goals in mind as they participate in development of these new capabilities.

The ARL North American Interlibrary Loan/Document Delivery Project described by Mary Jackson is an example of where those public objectives are clear. The project's purpose is to reconceptualize interlibrary loan and document delivery–to create efficiencies in the delivery of information in order to reduce costs to libraries by automating a still heavily manual interlibrary loan process and to speed delivery to patrons by utilizing new technologies. The project also assumes use of commercial document suppliers where those services are cheaper than what can be provided by libraries, so that libraries can focus on those materials important to scholarship but without significant commercial value. The systems design will provide for flexibility as to whether libraries pass none, some, or all of these costs on to their patrons; but the ability not to do so will be provided at the request of many public institutions and consortia. Information about this project has been shared widely with other organizations and associations in the library and information field in order to have maximum support of the outcome at the national level. To that extent, this project serves as a model for how new definitions of core services and value-added services might also be pursued within the profession. Similarly, the ARL Electronic Reserves Project involves research libraries, publishers, and university bookstores in experiments on how the reserves function can be moved into an electronic environment.

ARE WE UP TO THE CHALLENGE?

Public universities and their research libraries do have an identifiable responsibility to serve the public good. Citizens and funding agencies expect them to honor that commitment. Given decreases in public funding suffered to date, rapidly changing technologies, rising user expectations, and the increasing commercialization of information, librarians from public research universities must proceed with determination to hold onto their principles and to be aggressive in demanding that those principles be reflected in the design of new information delivery systems. Scholarly communication is not well served by a model that only supports commercial exploitation of information. For these principles to be protected, librarians from public institutions must be directly involved in the development of new systems and services in order to help define the objectives and to evaluate whether these systems protect the public's interests. This will require a national presence and participation in many projects and developments over many years, as well as consistent and long term campus leadership. In addition to imagination, technical support, and talented staff, it will require leadership, determination, and stamina. Are we up to the challenge?

NOTES

1. Schmidt, Steffen. "Public Policy Issues Facing The University," in *Strategic Planning Position Papers*. Ames, Iowa State University of Science and Technology, March 1994. 35.

2. Simonson, Michael R. "Extended and Continuing Education: Resolving a Mission in Conflict–A Faculty Perspective," in *Strategic Planning Position Papers*. Ames, Iowa State University of Science and Technology, March 1994. 212, 219.

3. Kuuttila, Lisa. "University Partnerships for Technology Transfer: Industry, Community Colleges," in *Strategic Planning Position Papers*. Ames, Iowa State University of Science and Technology, March 1994. 236.

4. *ARL Statistics, 1992-93*. Washington, D.C., Association of Research Libraries, 1994. [4]-7, appendix.

5. *University Libraries and Scholarly Communication; a Study Prepared for the Andrew W. Mellon Foundation* by Anthony M. Cummings, Marcia L. Witte, William G. Bowne, Laura O. Lazarus, and Richard H. Ekman. Washington, D.C., Association of Research Libraries, November 1992. xvii, 23-40.

6. See such publications as: (a) *University Libraries and Scholarly Communications* (ARL, 1992); (b) *Association of American Universities Research Libraries Project: Reports of the AAU Task Forces on Acquisition and Distribution of Foreign Language and Area Studies Materials; A National Strategy for Managing Scientific and Technological Information; Intellectual Property Rights in an Electronic Environment* (ARL, 1994); (c) Hawkins, Brian. "Planning for the National Electronic Library," *Educom Review* 29, 3 (May/June 1994): 19-29; (d) Association of Research Libraries. *Strategy for the 1990s* (ARL, 1991); (e) Drabenstott, Karen M. *Analytical Review of the Library of the Future* (Council on Library Resources, 1994); (f) Clinton, William J. and Gore Jr., Albert. *Technology for America's Economic Growth: A New Direction to Build Economic*

38   *THE FUTURE OF RESOURCE SHARING*

Strength. Office of the President of the United States, February 22, 1993 [and subsequent elaborations on this topic in speeches by Vice President Gore, publications of federal agencies, and Congressional legislation]; and (g) publications of the Coalition for Networked Information, a coalition of member institutions from ARL, CAUSE, and EDUCOM.

    7. Hawkins, 22.

Real Access as the Paradigm
of the Nineties

Paul H. Mosher

THE AGE OF BIBLIOGRAPHIC ACCESSIBILITY

The automation of the card catalog and major internal library processes was the paradigm of research libraries' planning and vision for the period 1970-1990. This vision, of the "automated" library, in which redundant and detailed paper-based processes were converted to electronic form, was the culmination of a set of achievements, the object of which was to make universal bibliographic access a reality. It was an initiative as vast, and as visionary, as the Public Library Movement of the early Twentieth Century, or the great union catalog and interlibrary loan efforts which helped to shape the directions of librarianship in the years before and after the Second World War. Equally important has been the development of the Anglo-American Cataloging Rules which set standards for card catalog production that enabled the union catalog and interlibrary loan initiatives.

The goal of all this was to make existing knowledge as widely discoverable as possible, create widespread information accessibility through existing channels, and to automate library processing and circulation operations in order to reduce costs and speed availability.

Paul H. Mosher is Vice Provost and Director of Libraries at the University of Pennsylvania in Philadelphia, PA, where he also holds an Adjunct Professorship in History.

[Haworth co-indexing entry note]: *"Real* Access as the Paradigm of the Nineties." Mosher, Paul H. Co-published simultaneously in *Journal of Library Administration* (The Haworth Press, Inc.) Vol. 21, No. 1/2, 1995, pp. 39-48; and *The Future of Resource Sharing* (ed: Shirley K. Baker, and Mary E. Jackson) The Haworth Press, Inc., 1995, pp. 39-48. Multiple copies of this article/chapter may be purchased from The Haworth Document Delivery Center [1-800-342-9678; 9:00 a.m. - 5:00 p.m. (EST)].

© 1995 by The Haworth Press, Inc. All rights reserved.

40 THE FUTURE OF RESOURCE SHARING

While the goal of completely integrated electronic library processing and management has not been attained fully yet, the integrated library systems that began to appear in the late 1970s, such as CLSI, Geac, NOTIS and VTLS transformed technical operations, serials processing, the catalog and circulation in fundamental ways.[1]

Paper processes became largely automated–if minimally redesigned–and vast electronic union catalogs which we have come to call "utilities" (e.g., RLIN, OCLC) came into being as a partial outcome. The invention of "copy cataloging," the process by which libraries derive their own catalog records electronically from those originally created elsewhere, was a profound technical innovation, and transformed a large segment of the catalog process–it has proved a model for the kinds of changes we hope to achieve elsewhere in our organizations by the application of electronic modalities.

With the new systems introduced in the 1980s, and the refinement and upgrade of some of the older systems, a revolution in library operations has been achieved. The revolution is not yet complete, of course; revolutions never are. In addition to a progressive set of improvements and refinements, of which the most important may be the creation of online catalogs and linking of the serials and circulation files to catalog records, integrated library systems must now enable the automated paper processes to be transformed into simplified, less redundant, more economic and efficient electronic processes.

THE COSTS OF ACCESS:
THE NEW CRISIS OF THE NINETIES

While the volume of new publications increases exponentially (a trend complicated by the increase in formats, media, and technologies), and the cost of those materials increases geometrically, the financial resources available for libraries to acquire them increase only arithmetically (see Figure 1). As we all know, this cost algorithm has been led by the skyrocketing costs of key serials in certain disciplines, especially the sciences, technology, and medicine. Ironically, most information published in the journals with the steepest cost increases is generated by our own scholars, heavily subsidized, in most cases, by our universities, which are then confronted with

FIGURE 1. The Principal Factors Affecting Library Programs (1990-2000)

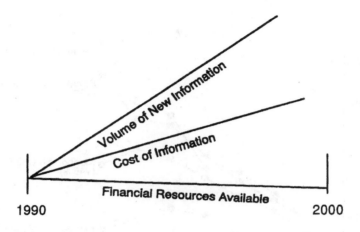

the galling necessity of buying their information back again, at very high cost.

The gap between the available financial resources and the amount of new knowledge, information and data is growing. Each of our libraries is acquiring fewer materials for significantly more money than a decade ago. The Association of Research Libraries has captured this trend effectively in a now-famous graph (Figure 2).[2]

The impact of this trend is the rapid growth of interlibrary loan traffic: in the decade between 1982 and 1992, lending traffic increased 52%, while borrowing traffic increased 108% among ARL libraries (Figure 3).[4]

In 1983, ARL libraries reported 2,020,743 loans and 738,905 borrows, while ten years later, these figures had increased to 3,231,985 loans and 1,490,494 borrows. The total cost of 1993 traffic in 1993 dollars was $63,694,945 based on the ARL/RLG figures–a figure which represents nearly 11% of the total amount spent on acquisitions by ARL libraries in that year.[5]

At present, demand for these resources is growing rapidly, and provision is very reliable–our traditional interlibrary loan processes work well in terms of dependability. But they are costly at an average of $29.55 per transaction plus an undetermined cost to

FIGURE 2. Monograph and Serial Costs in ARL Libraries (1986-1993)

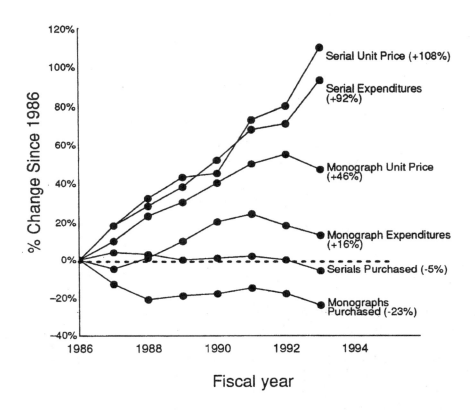

Source: *ARL Statistics, 1992-93*. Prepared by Kendon Stubbs; copyright 1994 by the Assocation of Research Libraries and reprinted here with permission.

users. Faculty and students would argue that the institutional costs are paltry compared with the costs they incur in trying to obtain delivery of materials unavailable locally. These costs are real, and should be calculated in any serious effort to understand the full institutional costs of interlibrary borrowing. (I wonder how much more time could be devoted to teaching or other productive endeavors if a large part of the collective effort devoted by faculty to obtaining interlibrary loan could be redirected?) In many cases, as well, the processes are too slow.[6]

FIGURE 3. Resources per Student in ARL Libraries (1986-1993)

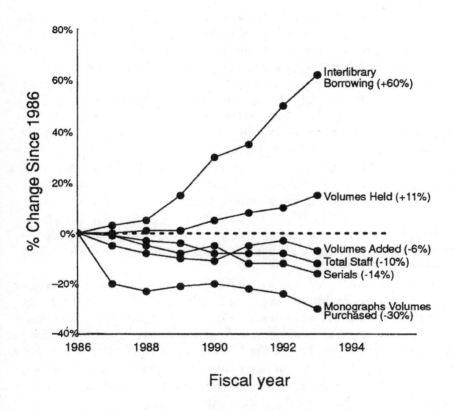

Note: The total student population has increased 11% since 1986. This graph compares the growth in number of students with changes in interlibrary borrowing, library staff, and acquisitions.

Source: *ARL Statistics, 1992-93*. Prepared by Kendon Stubbs; copyright 1994 by the Assocation of Research Libraries and reprinted here with permission.

The entire set of processes and operations involved in ILL–by both staff and requesters–are staff- and paper-intensive operations that are surpassing demand rates that can be handled effectively using traditional systems. The traditional systems, which served us well for years, are breaking down and are in urgent need of redesign.

ACCESS vs. OWNERSHIP: THE VIRTUAL LIBRARY

Libraries have recently been passing through a period in which they saw access as opposed to ownership as the shaping paradigm of cost-management during the eighties. In this paradigm, the concept of "comprehensive" paper library collections (which for many meant buy everything you can, whether used or not), would give way to a "Virtual Library" in which the collections of all would be shared by all, and in which conventional ownership would be replaced by interlibrary borrowing of one kind or another, and by pay-as-you-go document suppliers.

In this model, the new access enabled by the automation of bibliographic records would be isomorphically transformed into electronic access to all information, wherever it would be stored. Thus, libraries felt justified in transforming collection dollars to automation dollars, since the new networks, consortia and document delivery services were seen to offer an alternative construct to ownership.

But development of the Virtual Library has encountered problems—economic, technical, legal, and cultural—that have delayed its development, and it has evolved in new and unforeseen directions. It may be regarded as another manifestation of the "paradigm drift" described by the president of the University of Rochester at a recent ACLS meeting.[7] New technology does not replace old technology, but supplements or layers it in unforeseen ways, and may add to existing costs rather than displace them.

Although the most obvious gap-bridging solution presented in Figure 1 is resource sharing, the costs of the present ILL system defeat the potential economic benefits of sharing resources. The procedures themselves often remain complex, detailed and redundant—thus staff-intensive and, *ipso facto*, expensive. Document delivery services, while often efficient and rapid, add layers of cost, including copyright payments, and usually can only supply titles from "core" lists which are heavily in demand, and thus subject to rights compensation, as well as adding overhead costs that may include return of a profit margin to ownership. Thus, document delivery services supplement, rather than replace, traditional borrowing processes. Finally, ILL, if not document supply services, can be too slow.

Furthermore, someone must have the information before a patron can "access" it. Part of the magic underlying the "Virtual Library" concept is the aggregate richness of the knowledge and information resources gathered over centuries by the country's research, special, and public libraries. But if we stop collecting, and trade our collections dollars for access technology, will we have thrown away the meat in the electronic sandwich?[8] Planning, collaboration, and communication in the area of collection development and management are vital parts of the substructure necessary before effective resource sharing can take place.

In the interlibrary reform marketplace, it is sometimes easy to fall into an unfortunate isomorphic transformation of words: just as the terms "information," "knowledge" and "technology" have distinct meanings which must be remembered, "virtual" is a word that can hide important realities. Our goal as librarians remains the real, timely delivery of knowledge and information. "Virtual information" is an oxymoron.

PLOTTING THE INFORMATION FUTURE

Within this complex and distributed information future, alliances and coalitions must be formed and contractual arrangements made, to enable our users the best, easiest, cheapest, most friendly and consistent possible access. Each of our libraries will construct a pattern of information access and delivery that conforms to its own constituent goals, needs and culture, and to the influence of the marketplace. Within the complex of structures, market, economic and cultural pressures will encourage the growth and spread of more effective structures and components, and the withering or failure of others. Effective resource sharing, hitherto elusive over the long run, is an unavoidable price of wider distribution of information resources.

The processing revolution, which led to substantial efficiencies in technical services, catalog access, and circulation, was the paradigm of change over the last twenty years. The tools created by this wave of change and improvement have been supplemented by supplementing the electronic catalogs with index and abstract tools and access to shared utilities such as OCLC and RLIN, which bring

THE FUTURE OF RESOURCE SHARING

union access to collections of other libraries. The complex of new electronic tools brings infinitely improved and extended user and staff access to available knowledge, information and data resources. But the new complex of resources, which represents the core of an electronic reference room in the electronic library, has brought with it a range of new issues and problems which must be addressed in a collaborative and cooperative arena.

BEYOND ACCESS:
REVOLUTIONIZING DOCUMENT DELIVERY

The library paradigm for the 1990s must be the creation of new delivery structures which capitalize on the access tools and structures created by librarians during the past generation. They must be faster and cheaper, and handle increasing volumes of activity. Librarians have already begun the process: major utilities are improving their ILL components, by which requests are electronically transmitted among libraries; and there is urgent need for linking them so that documents can be requested by a single process through any utility which contains them. Some libraries are experimenting with electronic requesting of loans via e-mail to local ILL offices, and these are important steps. But they are not enough.

More widespread user self-service–in the form of user-initiated electronic request tools based on holdings records derived from major utilities, server-supported electronic forms generation and processing, pre-programmed routing protocols, electronic document delivery systems linked directly to delivery requests, electronically and automatically generated management and fiscal data and direct user delivery systems–are key components of an improved document-delivery future. As is always the case with new electronic systems, there will be crucial tradeoffs between cost reduction and improved functionality. Ideally, system variations will allow local decision-makers choices which would optimize system applications to their local circumstances.

Hopefully, this process will parallel the successes of Coalition for Networked Information to transform the nature of scholarly scientific publication and its costs, and to recapture for scholars the legacy of the information they have themselves created but which they must often re-acquire at prohibitive cost. Together, the reforms of creation, distribution, access, and delivery of scholarly "publications," if successful, may enable us to seize and redirect to more productive purposes the massive energy and financial resources presently lost to the inefficiencies and redundancy of the processes as they now exist.

If the transformation of technical processing was the change paradigm for libraries in the 1970s and 1980s, transformation of the delivery of information resources among libraries, capitalizing on the earlier set of accomplishments, must be the major goal of libraries in the 1990s. Effective delivery equals *real* access. We must harness the strengths of electronics to achieve request and delivery mechanisms so simple and easy that our users will wonder why they didn't always exist. The processes must be so simple that they revolutionize both the costs of ILL and its functionalities. The new delivery paradigm must effectively solve the demand paradox illustrated in Figure 1.

The process of change we outline above will call for further change in our organizations—the testing of the present structure and the called-for redesign will require *real* resource sharing, to assure *real* access. Thus, resource sharing must be undertaken to support wide access to information not otherwise available, not as a substitute for acquiring adequate information levels for the curriculum or for the library's basic mission. The changes are called for to support advanced inquiry and research nationally and internationally, and have the potential for supporting true universal access to publications, even as we achieve more effective management and control of costs.

AUTHOR NOTE

Paul Mosher completed a PhD at the University of California, Berkeley, in 1969. He was Deputy Director at Stanford University before moving to Penn in 1988. He is active in the American Library Association, in which he has held a number of offices, and the Association of Research Libraries, and is Chairman of the Board of the Research Libraries Group. Dr. Mosher has written and lectured extensively on Collection Development and Collection Management. In addition to his duties as University Librarian, he is a frequent advisor to libraries and foundations throughout the United States, Canada, Europe, Australia and New Zealand.

NOTES

1. See William Saffady, "Integrated Library Systems for Minicomputers and Mainframes: A Vendor Study. Part I." *Library Technology Reports*, 30 (1), Feb., 1994, pp. 9-11.

2. *ARL Statistics, 1992-93*, p. 6. The implication of this trend for smaller libraries, which bear increasing demand from larger libraries, has yet to be explored.

3. Marilyn M. Roche, *ARL/RLG Interlibrary Loan Cost Study. A Joint Effort by the Association of Research Libraries and the Research Libraries Group.* Washington, Association of Research Libraries, 1993, p. iv.

4. *ARL Statistics, 1992-93*, p. 6. The implication of this trend for smaller libraries, which bear increasing demand from larger libraries, has yet to be explored.

5. Roche, *Interlibrary Loan Cost Study*, p. iv. The 1993 materials cost data are from *ARL Statistics, 1992-93*, p. 32.

6. An average of eleven days for the Penn Library.

7. Presentation by President Dennis O'Brien of the University of Rochester, in a panel on "Knowledge for What (and for whom)?" at the 75th Annual Meeting of the American Council of Learned Societies, Philadelphia, April 29, 1994.

8. To borrow a useful metaphor coined by Patricia Battin.

Scholarly Publishing, Copyright, and the Future of Resource Sharing

William Gray Potter

The Congress shall have power . . . To promote the progress of science and useful arts, by securing for limited times to authors and inventors the exclusive right to their respective writings and discoveries . . . (U.S. Constitution, Article 1, Section 8)

PURPOSE OF COPYRIGHT

As the constitution states, Congress is authorized to establish copyright laws to promote "the progress of science and useful arts." The basic function of copyright, then, is not to reward the author or the publisher but rather to encourage the dissemination of ideas. Justice Sandra Day O'Connor expressed this well in a 1991 opinion:

> The primary objective of copyright is not to reward the labour of authors, but [t]o promote the Progress of Science and useful arts. To this end, copyright assures authors the right to their original expression, but encourages others to build freely upon the ideas and information conveyed by a work. The result is

---

William Gray Potter is Director of Libraries at the University of Georgia in Athens, GA.

[Haworth co-indexing entry note]: "Scholarly Publishing, Copyright, and the Future of Resource Sharing." Potter, William Gray. Co-published simultaneously in *Journal of Library Administration* (The Haworth Press, Inc.) Vol. 21, No. 1/2, 1995, pp. 49-66; and *The Future of Resource Sharing* (ed: Shirley K. Baker, and Mary E. Jackson) The Haworth Press, Inc., 1995, pp. 49-66. Multiple copies of this article/chapter may be purchased from The Haworth Document Delivery Center [1-800-342-9678; 9:00 a.m. - 5:00 p.m. (EST)].

© 1995 by The Haworth Press, Inc. All rights reserved.

50 THE FUTURE OF RESOURCE SHARING

neither unfair nor unfortunate. It is the means by which copyright advances the progress of science and art.[1]

The membership of the Association of Research Libraries has adopted a statement affirming both the rights and the responsibilities of the research library community that states: "The genius of the United States copyright law is that it balances the intellectual property rights of authors, publishers, and copyright owners with society's need for the free exchange of ideas."[2]

To advance knowledge and to ensure the free exchange of ideas, U.S. law and court decisions have long limited the monopoly that the copyright holder has over the expression and distribution of a work. Under the U.S. Copyright Act of 1976, libraries are given the right to reproduce materials for several purposes. Most pertinent here, under section 108 of the Act, a library can make a copy of an article for a reader and can enter into routine interlibrary loan arrangements. In addition, the 1976 Act recognizes the concept of fair use, permitting copying of works for such purposes as teaching, scholarship, and research as long as certain criteria are met.

Copyright, then, does not grant the holder an absolute monopoly on the expression or communication of a work. Rather, it grants the holder a limited monopoly with certain exemptions for purposes that advance knowledge, including copying by libraries and by users. Much of the basis for these exemptions is common sense. A faculty member finds an article of interest and, rather than reading it in the library, makes a photocopy so he can read it later. There is no loss of revenue to the copyright holder because the alternative would have been for the faculty member to read the article in the library. Even more basic is the recognition by Congress and the courts that providing exemptions for the use of works for teaching, scholarship and research does more to "promote the progress of science and useful arts" than would an absolute monopoly. In other words, the law attempts to strike the best balance possible.

This balance would work well if the weights at either end were inert. The truth is that the weights are alive and squirming, and always trying to tip the balance. Readers and libraries, representing readers, will always push for the greatest possible access. Publishers, as the holder of the copyright, will always push for the greatest restrictions on use because that provides the largest possible return. To be fair, both sides promote the advancement of knowledge. Readers and libraries do so by pushing for the maximum flow of information. Publishers do so by stressing that they must have a certain level of return on their investment if they are to stay in business. The law attempts to provide both an appropriate level of free exchange and an appropriate return for the copyright holder. However, it is not surprising that the parties at either end of the beam do not always agree.

Section 108(g)(2) of the 1976 Copyright Act expressly states that libraries are not prevented from entering into interlibrary loan arrangements as long as the receiving library does not receive copies "in such aggregate quantities as to substitute for a subscription to or purchase of" a work. The National Commission on New Technological Uses of Copyrighted Works (CONTU) consulted with libraries and publishers and developed guidelines for what might constitute "such aggregate quantities." The essential component of these guidelines is that within a single calendar year, a library should not borrow more than five articles from the most recent five years of publication of a journal. If more are needed, then the library should subscribe to the journal, seek permission, or pay a fee. Most libraries have adopted these guidelines and they have proved workable. Experience at the University of Georgia is that the CONTU guidelines allow the library to borrow an adequate number of copies from journals not held locally. If more than five articles are needed from a journal, this is usually a good sign that a subscription is needed. This happens so rarely that funds for a subscription can usually be identified, sometimes by canceling another journal that is receiving less use.

Ironically, the original purpose of copyright was to protect authors from unscrupulous publishers who would pirate their books. Today, in scholarly publishing, it is more often invoked to protect publishers who have stipulated that the copyright be assigned to them as a condition of publication. Most authors readily do this. Their chief objective is to publish because, as faculty members, they are rewarded for publishing by their institution. Therefore, compensation to the author or to the author's employer is only rarely an issue. The author, with the employer's assent, signs the copyright over to the publisher. While this might be perceived as inequitable, it has become an accepted component of the current system of scholarly publishing. Thus, the purpose of copyright has moved from protecting the author to protecting the publisher. The publishers argue that the only way they can profitably publish scholarly journals is to assume the copyright and then rigorously enforce it. If this is true, then, under the current system, the promotion of science and useful arts has come to depend upon the assignment of copyright to the publishers.

IMPORTANCE OF SCHOLARLY JOURNALS

When considering copyright and resource sharing in academic libraries, the real concern is with scholarly publishing. While academic libraries lend novels, trade books, and copies of articles from general periodicals, these activities are not the focus of resource sharing among them. Rather, publications resulting from scholarly endeavors, chiefly by university faculty, are the central issue. More specifically, the concern is with scholarly journals, especially in the sciences. Thus, it is appropriate to concentrate upon scholarly journals when considering copyright and the future of resource sharing among academic libraries.

Even more to the point, it is the expensive journals that are of most concern. Libraries need to share that which is in short supply. The materials that are in short supply are either old, obscure, or expensive. The old and obscure items can usually be shared freely without concern of copyright either because the content has passed into the public domain or because the producer is not concerned with commercial exploitation. It is the journals that are rare because they are expensive that are of the greatest concern. If only a few libraries can afford to subscribe to a journal, then other libraries will turn to those few when an article is needed from that journal. At the same time, because the journal is expensive, the publisher will be most concerned about possible lost revenues.

Perhaps the most critical problem facing academic and research libraries today is how to provide articles from expensive journals when budgets allow them to subscribe to fewer of these journals each year. Traditional interlibrary loan is one solution and one that is permitted under the fair use provisions of the copyright law. Libraries and publishers have established guidelines for interlibrary lending that have been proven to work fairly well. However, traditional interlibrary lending is too slow and perhaps too expensive for delivering the content of these journals. Instead, libraries have turned to expedited interlibrary programs and to commercial services. To date, though, nothing is as satisfactory as subscribing to the journal.

Still, libraries look for new solutions out of necessity. The current state of journal publishing is breaking the backs of academic libraries. They simply cannot keep pace with cost increases. However, solutions that libraries develop are often in conflict with the publishers who own the copyright to these journals, especially when those solutions involve sharing among libraries. This essay will attempt to explain the libraries' perspective on this crucial problem by first looking at how the current system of scholarly journal publishing evolved over the past fifty years followed by a detailed look at the shortcomings of the current system. For the system to improve, attitudes and perceptions will have to change and these needed changes will be discussed as well. Finally, the implications of an improved system of scholarly communication upon copyright and resource sharing will be discussed.

GROWTH OF SCHOLARLY JOURNAL PUBLISHING

The current system of scholarly publishing developed over the past 50 years. Prior to World War II, most scholarly journals were published by learned societies and universities. This was not seen as a profit making enterprise but rather a means to disseminate knowledge among scholars. It was a professional obligation to ensure that learned work was made available and copyright was rarely a concern. The system of an editor, an editorial board, and the use of blind referees to determine what would be published was and is a long established practice. Distribution was straightforward and marketing non-existent since society members and libraries were the primary subscribers.

After World War II, spending for research and education accelerated. There were soon more faculty and researchers seeking outlets to publish their work. Moreover, new fields of research and subspecialties were appearing. At the same time, funding for libraries improved dramatically. Commercial publishers began to see a market that had not existed before.[3] Established publishers like Wiley, Blackwells, and Elsevier either acquired journals from learned societies or started their own. Robert Maxwell started Pergamon Press to publish scholarly journals in specialized fields and made enough money to build a great media empire.[4]

The formula used by these commercial publishers was simple. Identify an area where work was being done but where no journal yet existed or where there was not enough space in existing journals. The amount of knowledge that needed to be recorded and published was growing exponentially and the authors had to publish in order to get tenure or to fulfill the terms of their grants. Editors and editorial boards were willing to work for little compensation because of the prestige of working on a respected journal and because they were rewarded by their employers. Libraries were well funded and willing to try just about any journal. Also, faculty were clamoring for journals tailored to their fields of research. For commercial publishers, this was a real opportunity and they served a vital purpose. They provided the capital, the copyediting, the typesetting, the production, the distribution, and the marketing at a time when no one else could do it. While they made considerable profits, they were willing to invest in starting more new journals in other emerging fields. They were also busy seeking the rights to publish the more established journals of the learned societies, many of which were swayed by the promise of increased income, income that often came from higher subscription rates for libraries.

It is widely recognized that the number of serials has been growing dramatically for the past fifty years. The most often cited figures indicate that the number of serials has grown from 70,000 in 1972 to over 110,000 by 1987. During the same time period, the median purchase price of serials increased by 350 percent.[5]

Publishers found that authors and universities were not concerned about retaining copyright. Obtaining some financial return on publication was not a concern for authors or for the employer. The publishers found that they could request that the copyright be turned over to them as a condition of publication. Libraries did not object to this because copyright had rarely been an issue for them either.

Academic libraries and, to a lesser extent, special libraries have long been the primary subscribers to scholarly journals.[6] Through-out the 1950s and 1960s, their budgets expanded to keep pace with any cost increases. In the early 1970s, research libraries began to lose purchasing power due largely to the fact that the dollar was released to float against other currencies. Considerable concern was expressed about the escalating costs of scholarly journals in the early to mid 1970s.[7] During the late 1970s and early 1980s, this concern diminished. Then, academic library budgets began to con-tract as cost increases escalated. At first, funds were diverted from purchasing monographs but, as publishers began to increase costs beyond the rate of inflation, libraries began to cancel journals. Accus-tomed to substantial returns, the publishers reacted by increasing their prices even more which resulted in more cancellations. The publishers raised rates to recover lost revenues and to continue expansion. This resulted in more cancellations and in the vicious cycle that continues today.

Hard times have forced many to look at the current system for scholarly publishing and, when examined with a critical eye, there are many problems.

SHORTCOMINGS IN EXISTING SYSTEM OF SCHOLARLY PUBLISHING

The production cycle of a journal article can be seen as a chain with many links–author, editor, reviewer, copyeditor, typesetter, publisher, library, indexer, and finally reader. Only two of the links in this chain are essential–the author and the reader. All the rest are middlemen, working to connect the reader and the author. It is only appropriate that the production cycle be examined and, if appropri-ate, re-engineered.

There are several inequities and inefficiencies in the current state of journal publishing, but nine jump out as the most egregious. These are problems that center around the more expensive journals, especially in the sciences. While these journals account for a small percentage of the number of titles received, they do absorb the majority of a library's budget for journals.

Value Added and Financial Reward Not Connected

The value of a journal article really comes from the author, editor, and editorial board, who are usually unpaid volunteers in the process. The author writes an article and submits it to an editor. The editor receives it and sends it to one or more reviewers. Together, the editor and reviewer act as gatekeepers who may reject, accept, or ask for substantial changes in the article. The intellectual work is performed by these people. Once accepted, the paper is sent to the publisher for copyediting, typesetting, publication, and distribution. While these are certainly valuable activities, they do not compare to the effort of writing or the value of the experts who reviewed the article. However, any significant financial reward goes to the publisher.

Two important elements missing from the discussion so far are the employing institution, often a university, and the agency that funded the research upon which the article is based, usually a government agency. To date, employers and funding agencies have not been concerned with revenue that derives from work performed by authors, editors, and reviewers. However, as finances become increasingly scarce and as legislators and citizens ask increasingly hard questions about the value of research, this is an area that bears examination. Consider also that the primary purchasers of these journals are the libraries of the same institutions that employ the author, editor, and reviewers.

The judge in the recent Texaco copyright case made an interesting statement in his opinion. He said "The profit motive is the engine that ensures the progress of science."[8] The publishers were, of course, delighted by this. The problem is, though, that the profit motive did not lead the university to employ the author, the government to fund the research, the author to write the article, the editor to edit the journal, or the referee to review the article. The real intellectual work, the essential value of the article, is not motivated by profit and is not directly rewarded.

Time Delay

Especially in the sciences, the delay involved in getting an article from the author to the reader is often too long.[9] In many fields, especially ones where the number of researchers at the cutting edge is fairly small, this time lag has been addressed through the sharing of pre-prints or typescript copies of the papers. More recently, these pre-prints have been made available across the Internet.[10]

Sophisticated Secondary Access, Rudimentary Primary Access

Under the current system, libraries provide highly sophisticated access to secondary sources, that is to abstracting and indexing services, using computerized systems. At many institutions, researchers can find citations and abstracts very quickly and often at no direct charge because the library has mounted databases for them to use. However, once a citation is found in one of these databases, the act of acquiring the article is cumbersome. Even if the library subscribes to the journal, the reader must locate the item, go to where it is shelved, and read or photocopy it. If the library does not own it, then the reader must request it on interlibrary loan or through a commercial document delivery service. The contrast between the highly sophisticated access to bibliographic citations and the rudimentary access to the actual article emphasizes the shortcomings of the current system and is driving readers to ask for better delivery systems.

Prevailing Interpretation of Copyright

The current, prevailing interpretation of copyright in the U.S. makes publishers' rights supreme. Yet, the Constitution grants Congress the power to make copyright and patent laws for the protection of the author or inventor and the advancement of knowledge. There is no mention of publisher. The basic problem is that the system today expects authors to sign copyright over to the publisher.

Economic Colonialism

The raw material, the actual research, of most journal articles is performed by faculty at universities or researchers at government facilities. This raw material is turned into an article by the author, reviewed and vetted by colleagues and, in effect, the final product is then ready except for the fit and finish of copyediting and the

58 THE FUTURE OF RESOURCE SHARING

packaging of publishing. Yet, at this point, the article is turned over to a publisher who then sells the article back to the libraries of the same universities. Economically, this is dysfunctional and is reminiscent of colonialism where colonial powers removed raw materials with little compensation, converted these materials to products, and then sold them back to the colonies.

Unfair Subsidy for Publishers

Looking at this another way, the current system provides an unfair subsidy to the publisher. The articles, the basic material of their journals, are written, edited, and reviewed by faculty and researchers, often with public funds, and then repurchased by libraries, again often with public funds. In effect, the universities and the government are giving the product away to publishers and then buying it back.

Few Articles Are Actually Read

Libraries purchase, bind, and shelve journals and pay for access to the abstracting and indexing services that allow readers to find the articles they need. However, only a few of the articles in any given issue of a journal are ever read by the library's particular clientele. So, whole journals are purchased when only a few articles are needed.[11]

Not First Choice for Information

For all its expense, this system of scholarly communication is not the reader's or researcher's first choice for finding information. Libraries spend considerable sums to purchase and shelve journals and to provide indexing to these journals. Yet, studies show that when a scientist needs information, the first source of choice is an office collection followed by colleagues.[12] In many fields, the information in journals is out of date by the time it is published or the scientist has already learned of it through pre-prints or from the Internet. For graduate students and younger faculty, the library is the chief source of information, but as they progress in their field and become more specialized, they tend to have the journals they need in their offices and they build relationships with colleagues that are all the easier to maintain on the Internet. The library collection is of most use to them when they venture outside of their specialty.

Too Expensive

The last and most damning problem with the current system of scholarly journals is the fact that it is simply too expensive. It is expensive now and prices continue to escalate. We could probably live with the other problems enumerated above if the journals were not so costly. At the University of Georgia, the average cost of a journal subscription has gone from $86 in 1985 to $210 in 1994 and we expect that they will increase at least another 10% in 1995.

IMPACT OF EXPENSIVE JOURNALS

Despite these criticisms and problems, the system does work for many journals, even for whole disciplines, especially in the social sciences and humanities. It works because the journals are not very expensive and are widely available. Also, for core journals, those 1,500 or so that are vital to undergraduate education, these shortcomings are more than compensated by the high use they receive. However, for many of the expensive scholarly journals, those needed for faculty and graduate research, especially in the sciences, these criticisms are valid. The system does not work. It is too expensive, it is too slow and it centers around producing, distributing, and storing a physical item when, in fact, it is the content, not the artifact that is important.

During fiscal year 1994, the University of Georgia Libraries spent about $2.5 million on journals. For this, we received about 12,000 journals. Analysis shows that 75 percent of the money went for 25 percent of the titles. In other words, $1,875,000 was spent to acquire just 3,000 journals while the remaining 9,000 titles were purchased for just $625,000. Further, one-fourth of the money, $625,000, went for just 300 titles or 2.5 percent of the list. So, at one end, one-fourth of the money purchased the 300 most expensive titles or 2.5 percent of the list while at the other end one-fourth of the money purchased 9,000 titles or 75 percent of the list. Earlier studies have found similar results.[13] Admittedly, market forces have been a major factor in driving these prices up and many of these journals are essential to academic and research programs. However, when one considers the problems with scholarly publishing, it is the expensive titles that need to be examined because that is where the bulk of the money is spent.

Virtually all of these expensive journals are scientific journals. Further, they are produced by a handful of publishers. At Georgia in 1994, five publishers combined received almost $750,000 for scientific journals, well over half of the total budgeted for journals in the sciences. These publishers are Elsevier/Pergamon, Springer, Wiley, Academic, and Kluwer. Moreover, one publisher, Elsevier, received almost $425,000 for science journals in fiscal year 1994, including Pergamon Press titles.[14]

The problems libraries face with access to scholarly journals are focused on the high end journals. These are the expensive journals that are being canceled and becoming scarce. Thus, libraries must turn to interlibrary loan or document delivery to provide access, often running headlong into publishers' concerns about copyright. If an alternate system of delivering scholarly information is to be developed and funded, it will likely come at the high end where significant funds are being expended and could be re-allocated. These expensive titles are the ones that need to be examined when one considers how scholarly publishing might be revamped. It does not make much sense to look at the journals that cost an average of $70. It makes more sense to look at the ones that average $625 or even $2,000.

Focusing on the high end journals, then, might offer the greatest return on an investment of time and money in a new system. Also, only a handful of publishers are involved, making the task more manageable. Three-fourths of our budgets for journals are being spent on just one-fourth of the titles and with only a few publishers. It makes considerable sense to focus on these journals and these publishers when considering ways to replace the current system, whether through improved resource sharing arrangements or document delivery or any system that is eventually developed to replace the established print journal.

NEEDED CHANGES

The problems with scholarly journals outlined above are not new. Libraries have been well aware of them for years and have been looking for solutions. The undergirding belief is that the paper journal will be replaced by an electronic system when it is economically and socially possible to do so. This will vary by journal and by discipline.

It should also be pointed out that even before the prevalence of computers and the advent of the Internet, systems were proposed that, in effect, advocated assembling papers or articles at a few distribution points and widely disseminating abstracts to the papers available at those distribution points. Bernal advocated such a system as early as 1939.[15] The National Institutes of Health undertook a program in the 1960s called the Information Exchange Group (IEG) experiment that attempted to formalize the distribution of papers among scientists.[16] In 1974, Hugh Atkinson outlined a system whereby the editorial apparatus of journals would continue but, instead of being set to type, edited typescript would be filmed and used to produce articles on demand with forty-eight hour turnaround.[17] Atkinson also saw the need for better abstracting and the possibility of paying a copyright fee for each article.

The need for an alternative system, then, has long been seen. As Houghton put it in 1975:

> Most of the criticisms launched at the scientific journal arise from the fact that the journal is a dilatory, expensive and unwieldy assemblage of papers. The alternatives that have been offered to replace the journal are in the main alternatives to the journal as a package of papers.[18]

Houghton goes on to state that the journal also has value as a collection of related papers and that the serendipity factor is vital, if immeasurable. In any event, the shortcomings of scholarly journals, especially in the sciences, have long been noted. They are slow and they are expensive. Today, the combination of computers and telecommunications makes it possible to look at more advanced solutions.

62   THE FUTURE OF RESOURCE SHARING

There are many models of what a system using networked computers might look like.[19] The details vary, but essentially authors would write papers and then submit them to an editor electronically over the network. The editor would send them to reviewers and, if the reception were favorable, the articles would be copyedited, formatted, and placed into a central database. Readers would search and find articles and then request them from the central database. Libraries would organize and archive this collection of electronic articles and, most important, subsidize the cost of access, possibly by reallocating funds now spent on print journals.[20]

Some variations have publishers playing a role. Others have the universities managing such a system. The details vary, but this is the general model many people see for delivering scholarly information in the future. It is essentially a "just in time" model versus the "just in case model" we now have. Libraries or the readers themselves would acquire the article when it is needed, just in time, versus buying it just in case it is needed.

What has to be there for this model to attain? The computer systems to do this and the networks connecting them are now in place. They may not be as sophisticated as they need to be, but the systems to do a good looking, electronic article database are there now. Indeed, there are several electronic journals published today that attempt to provide a refereed journal across the network.[21] However, the following problems need to be worked out before such a system can replace established scientific journals:

> *Economics.* It must be cheaper to obtain articles with this model than with the current system. If it must be cheaper, then it only makes sense that there is more of a margin for experimentation with a journal that now costs $2,500 than one that costs $25.
>
> *Sociology.* Publishing in an electronic database needs to receive the same acceptance and same respect as publishing in print journals. Promotion and tenure committees need to accept articles published in this way and this might be a real stumbling block. Also, faculty do not appear to be ready to embrace electronic replacements for journals. Even those in high technology fields seem to prefer the printed journal.
>
> *Role of the publishers.* For better or for worse, a few commer-

cial publishers now dominate scholarly publishing. Unless universities and learned societies cut them out, they must be reckoned with.

Copyright. The issue of who holds and controls copyright is open to question. Will it continue to be a publisher or will the agency that supported the research retain the copyright or will the author hold onto it?

These are all economic, legal, social, or market problems. The technology is not at issue. Journal articles could be delivered using electronic means tomorrow if technology were the only concern.

FUTURE OF RESOURCE SHARING

Again, the emphasis in this discussion has been upon high end, expensive journals. These are the journals that are absorbing much of academic library budgets and these are the ones where high costs might provide some margin for experimentation with new means of delivery. It may make sense to deliver other, less costly journals by the same system, but initially the most pressing need for a solution is at this high end. The University of Georgia could reallocate the $625,000 spent on the most expensive 300 titles if a system could be provided that addressed the four problems listed above and that replaced those 300 journals. If other research libraries were to join in, an annual project budget of $20 million to $30 million could easily be developed.

What would such a system mean for resource sharing and copyright? It all depends on who holds the copyright. There are two extreme scenarios. The first would have the publishers continue to play the dominant role in disseminating knowledge. The second would have the universities assume this position. The real outcome would likely be in between.

If the publishers maintain their dominant role, then things would not change except that the publishers would have a system that meters use. Under the fair use provisions of the copyright law, there is no doubt that copying for interlibrary loan and resource sharing is permissible. The CONTU guidelines effectively state that a library can borrow up to five articles from a journal each year from the last five years of publication without question. Experience has shown that this works fairly well. If a library borrows more than five articles from a given journal in a year, then it should probably subscribe to the journal. There are enough journals in any sizable collection that are used less frequently that can be canceled and the money reallocated. So, if the publishers retain control, then fair use should provide for library access. However, because the articles would be provided as they are needed and use could be metered, the publisher could refuse to permit access to a subscribing library if the purpose is to send a copy of an article to another library. For the publisher, this is the real advantage of electronic access. Use can be metered and controlled. It is possible that consortial licenses could be available from the publishers as is the case now with abstracting and indexing databases.

If the universities assume control, then the common assumption is that access will be much less restricted. Universities would likely enter into reciprocal agreements with each other to provide access to articles written by each other's faculty and researchers. Further, a common network would have to be supported and a means to archive articles indefinitely would have to be worked out. So, resource sharing in this case becomes less a matter of sharing the content of articles and more a matter of providing the network and the means to archive publications. For what the universities own, there will be fewer restrictions on use and more emphasis on sharing.

CONCLUSION

In any event, libraries will continue to own physical items and will begin to offer access to more and more titles electronically. Budgets for journals will be diverted to electronic access, but this diversion will take place over a long period and only for certain types of materials, such as expensive journals that are not economical in print form. Parallel systems will be the rule for the foreseeable future.

The new systems described above are all partial solutions. They do not appear to satisfy reader needs as fully and completely as the traditional model of library service did. But then, as Pogo said, the past is not what it used to be. The truth is, the old model was not totally effective either. It was big and comfortable and understandable. It did not raise expectations the way new systems do. But it was not wholly satisfactory. In truth, the range of partial solutions we have now, incomplete as they are, are an improvement.

The future of libraries is likely to be one of partial solutions to complex problems. Rather than one general model, we will have several models, each one fitted for a particular information need. For some needs, especially in the humanities and for undergraduate instruction, the traditional library works very well, and is very affordable. Paper publication in many fields is efficient and economical. For other needs, more electronic solutions will be appropriate. To rely upon only one model would be a mistake. A library that does not embrace electronic solutions today is not providing adequate service to its readers. On the other hand, one that seeks to replace print in all cases is making a big, costly mistake. We need to provide the appropriate tool for the appropriate need.

The biggest problem facing academic libraries today is the high and escalating cost of scholarly journals, especially in the sciences. As shown above, these costs are concentrated on the high end journals, those that cost several hundred dollars and more. It is these journals that present the greatest problem for resource sharing because they are the ones that libraries have had to cancel and now must seek through interlibrary loan and because these are the ones that publishers most seek to protect by exercising their copyright. Publishers' concerns about copyright are focused on these journals. The greatest return on any investment of time and money by libraries would be gained by working cooperatively to change the current system of scholarly publishing that now results in these high priced journals that can soak up more than three-fourths of a research library's budget for journals while delivering only one-fourth of the titles. This is where the money can be found to reallocate for an improved system.

NOTES

1. Justice Sandra Day O'Connor, *Feist Publications Inc. v. Rural Telephone Service Company, Inc.*, 111 Supreme Court 1282 (1991).

2. "Intellectual Property: An Association of Research Libraries Statement of Principles," adopted by ARL Membership, May 1994.

3. Gordon Graham, "The Economics of Journal Publishing: A Publisher's View," in Karen Brookfield ed., *Scholarly Communications and Serials Prices* (London: Bowker-Saur, 1991), p. 42.

4. Roy Greenslade, *Maxwell: The rise and fall of Robert Maxwell and his empire* (Secaucus, NJ : Carol Pub. Group, 1992.)

5. Duane E. Webster, "The Economics of Journal Publishing: The Librarian's View," in Karen Brookfield ed., *Scholarly Communications and Serials Prices* (London: Bowker-Saur, 1991), p. 29.

6. Bernard Houghton, *Scientific Periodicals: Their Historical Development, Characteristics, and Control* (London: Bingley, 1975), pp. 35-36.

7. Ann Okerson, "Of the Making of Books There is No End," in *Report of the ARL Serials Prices Project* (Washington: Association of Research Libraries, 1989), p. 1.

8. American Geophysical Union v. Texaco Inc., 82 Federal Supplement 1 (U.S. District Court for the Southern District of New York) 1992.

9. *Scholarly Communication: The Report of the National Enquiry* (Baltimore: Johns Hopkins, 1979), p. 49.

10. Gary Taubes, "Publication by electronic mail takes physics by storm," *Science* 259 (February 26, 1993); pp. 1246-48.

11. Hugh C. Atkinson, "The Future of the Scholarly Journal," in Peter Spyers-Duran and Daniel Gore, editors, *Management Problems in Serials Work* (Westport, Conn.: Greenwood Press, 1974), pp. 115-117.

12. *Scholarly Communication: The Report of the National Enquiry* . . . pp. 44-45.

13. Okerson, p. 28.

14. The author wishes to thank Bill Loughner, Bibliographer for Mathematics and Physical Sciences at The University of Georgia, for his assistance in compiling these numbers.

15. J.D. Bernal, *The Social Function of Science* (London: Routledge, 1939).

16. Houghton, pp. 47-48.

17. Atkinson, pp. 118-119.

18. Houghton, p. 43.

19. "A National Strategy for Managing Scientific and Technical Information," in Association of American Universities Research Libraries Project. *Reports of AAU Task Forces* (Washington: Association of Research Libraries, 1994), pp. 43-98.

20. An excellent recent description of how a networked system might work is described in: Andrew M. Odlyzko, "Tragic loss or good riddance? The impending demise of traditional scholarly journals," *International Journal of Man-Machine Studies*, 1995 (in press); condensed version to appear to *Notices of the American Mathematical Society*, January 1995; URL=ftp://netlib.att.com/netlib/att/math/odlyzko/tragic.loss.Z

21. *Directory of Electronic Journals, Newsletters, and Academic Discussion Lists* (Washington: Association of Research Libraries, Office of Scientific and Academic Publishing, 1991-).

Future of Resource Sharing in Research Libraries

Jutta Reed-Scott

Resource sharing in research libraries is at a critical juncture. Libraries in the future will have to integrate an array of information technologies to create an information-sharing environment where the individual user can both find and have delivered the materials he or she needs. Resource sharing in the electronic environment will have to provide a variety of connection and access choices to extend user access to information that the library does not hold locally through linking to multiple information resources from a single workstation.

Resource sharing programs or cooperative collection development programs among research libraries have a long and positive history. The principal objectives of these programs are to increase timely access to materials users need and that are not available in the local collections, and to extend coverage by shifting costs through reduction of duplicate collections. These premises have undergirded resource sharing programs for more than half a century. Today, resource sharing programs are on the cusp of transformation.

The convergence of several trends is transforming the ways libraries share resources. Economic pressures, increased user demands for

---

Jutta Reed-Scott is Senior Program Officer at the Association of Research Libraries in Washington, DC.

[Haworth co-indexing entry note]: "Future of Resource Sharing in Research Libraries." Reed-Scott, Jutta. Co-published simultaneously in *Journal of Library Administration* (The Haworth Press, Inc.) Vol. 21, No. 1/2, 1995, pp. 67-75; and *The Future of Resource Sharing* (ed: Shirley K. Baker, and Mary E. Jackson) The Haworth Press, Inc., 1995, pp. 67-75. Multiple copies of this article/chapter may be purchased from The Haworth Document Delivery Center [1-800-342-9678; 9:00 a.m. - 5:00 p.m. (EST)].

© 1995 by The Haworth Press, Inc. All rights reserved.

library resources, and technological changes are powerful driving forces in restructuring research library collecting programs and in reshaping cooperative collection management strategies.

All research libraries faced financial stringency in the last decade due to rising costs of library materials, the additional expenses for technology, and the university-wide economic pressures of balancing the budget. The 1992-93 statistics from the member libraries of the Association of Research Libraries present a disheartening picture of paying more for library materials and buying less. Prices for library materials continued to increase. The 1992-93 *ARL Statistics* show that 1993 expenditures for serials were almost twice as much as research libraries spent for serials in 1986, yet these libraries purchased 5% fewer serial titles than six years ago. The data show an equally steep increase in prices for monographs, with ARL university libraries buying 23% fewer monographs but paying 16% more in 1993 than in 1986.[1] The escalating costs of library materials as well as the budgetary constraints have steadily eroded research libraries' ability to build comprehensive, on-site collections. As the local resources have declined, resource sharing activities have increased substantially. The 106 member libraries of the Association of Research Libraries that have reported interlibrary loan statistics since 1986 showed that "borrowing rose from just under a million transactions to 1.4 million, or an increase of around 500,000. At the same time, for the same libraries, lending rose from 2.4 million to 3.1 million, an increase of 700,000."[2]

The most transforming factor is the rapid emergence and development of electronic information technologies that make it possible to envision different ways of organizing collections and services that libraries have traditionally provided. Information technologies will support new capacities for resource sharing and will allow distributed access. "Converging computing and telecommunications technologies have advanced to a point that they can now be deployed and integrated more effectively and economically than in the past."[3] Technological breakthroughs have also shifted greater computing power into the hands of end users. Students, faculty and other users on university campuses, equipped with their personal computers, can access myriad library catalogs on the Internet to locate resources not owned by the local library. As users gain access to information about collections, the demand for electronic access to the item will intensify. The extensive study, *University Libraries and Scholarly Communication,* captures the vision of user-initiated "direct access to the aggregate content of the nation's principal research collections, in which local and remote catalog entries and bibliographic records merge with readily retrieval electronic versions of full texts that can be downloaded and printed locally at one's own workstation."[4] The new technologies are fundamentally changing information access and they hold the promise of distributed, collaborative collection management on a scale that has not been possible before.

As research libraries plan for meeting the information needs of their students, faculty, researchers, and other users in the future, they face unprecedented opportunities and challenges. In the rapidly evolving environment of networked information, remote access, and desktop delivery, technology offers the potential for realizing a seamless web of interconnected, coordinated, and interdependent research collections that are accessible to geographically distributed users. Research libraries have extensive experience in sharing specialized research resources (obviating the need for duplicative investments) and in improving access to the growing universe of scholarly information resources. Information technologies can be used to enhance these resource sharing programs. There is no question that information technologies have enormous importance to managing library collections locally and in an interconnected networked environment, but the magnitude of the transformation is matched by the complexity of building the physical and organizational infrastructure.

On the most critical level, the full realization of distributed, networked research collections and of the new ways of scholarly communication depend "upon the development of an adequate national telecommunications infrastructure, capable of moving vast quantities of text and data at very high speeds."[5] Equally critically important is the implementation of the local campus networks to link scholars and researchers to the information highway. The development of this infrastructure will provide new ways of finding and obtaining research materials. It will give researchers access to research and will facilitate rapid delivery of electronic surrogates.

70   THE FUTURE OF RESOURCE SHARING

The organizational challenges of building the "North American digital library" are also daunting. The "digital library will consist of multiple forms and formats of information, including images, sounds, texts, computer programs, and quantitative data."[6] Equally important, it is no longer a single entity in a specific geographic location. " Instead it consists of resources that are constantly changing and available on a distributed basis."[7] How will libraries manage the transition to increased reliance on electronic networks for maximizing the collective information resources and to provide barrier-free access to those resources? Issues to be considered are:

- How should this "North American digital library" be structured?
- What are the user requirements in accessing remote collections electronically?
- What is the nature of the institutional commitment and role?
- What access methods are required and how will access service policies and standards be defined?
- How to balance and harmonize institutional user demands for onsite materials with the increasing dependence on remote access?
- What will be the impact of a broadened and enlarged user community on local collections?
- What strategies are needed to manage hybrid systems of print resources along with digitized materials?

There is an array of other issues that must be addressed including the technical requirements, capitalization of computing and communications technologies, funding of user access, funding of converting print resources to electronic format, and management of intellectual property issues.

INITIATIVES IN RESOURCE SHARING IN THE ELECTRONIC ENVIRONMENT

A number of current initiatives are testing the opportunities and challenges of moving to distributed, networked collections. On the national level, a catalyst for restructuring the ways of managing research collections in the electronic environment is the ARL/AAU Research Libraries Project that the Association of American Universities (AAU) initiated in 1993. The project was undertaken by AAU, an association of fifty-six American and two Canadian universities with strong programs of graduate and professional education and research, in collaboration with the Association of Research Libraries and with the support of The Andrew W. Mellon Foundation. As one component of the tripartite AAU Research Libraries Project, the AAU Task Force on Acquisition and Distribution of Foreign Language and Area Studies Materials was charged to develop and examine options for improving access to and delivery of foreign language materials. The Task Force has recommended the pursuit of a network-based, distributed program for coordinated collection development for foreign acquisitions. This Task Force recommendation calls for the implementation of a multi-institutional network of U.S. and Canadian research libraries that would share responsibility for collecting foreign imprint publications. The participating libraries would function as access nodes in a "distributed North American collection for foreign materials."[8] Such a multi-institutional network of coordinated collection building will require consensus and contractual agreements among research libraries and their constituent scholarly communities. One of the basic themes underlying the Task Force analysis is the vital importance of the electronic infrastructure to improve access to and delivery of information resources in foreign language, area and international studies. To test the barriers to distributed access and evaluate the impact of such a plan on the users of research library collections, three demonstration projects are proposed. The demonstration projects target research materials that originate in Latin America, Germany, and Japan.

Guiding the vision of the members of the Association of Research Libraries is the concept of a North American collaborative program where participating institutions share responsibility for collecting and delivering specialized–and initially primarily foreign language–research resources. The longterm goal is building a seamless web of interconnected, coordinated, and interdependent research collections that are electronically accessible to geographically distributed users. In such a networked, distributed collection, libraries

72 THE FUTURE OF RESOURCE SHARING

will play central roles as both providers of research materials as well as access points for users to these resources that will be increasingly in electronic form. Through shared planning and action, libraries will broaden the breadth and coverage of research resources in North American research libraries and serve as electronic gateways for ubiquitous access to these information resources. Coordinated collection management will ensure ownership in the research libraries community of materials needed as well as a networked access.

Realizing this vision of the North American digital library will allow research libraries to move to the "just-in-time" model of resource sharing while offering users "just-in-case" desktop access and delivery capabilities. It will also build the foundation for electronic resource sharing on a global basis.

On the regional level, the Committee on Institutional Cooperation (CIC) Libraries in the Midwest have launched a strategic planning initiative to create the "CIC Virtual Electronic Library." The vision outlined by CIC Library Directors is similar in spirit to the national program. It envisions that:

> By the beginning of the 21st Century, the CIC libraries will have a cohesive consortial organization guided by the vision of the information resources in the CIC as a seamless whole, whether those resources are developed or owned individually or collectively. Through shared planning and action the libraries and their patrons will have equal access to the total information resources of the CIC.[9]

For all libraries the challenge is how to manage the complex transition from print-based, institutional collections to greater reliance on digitized, shared resources.

THE FRAMEWORK FOR MOVING FORWARD

An important set of issues focuses on how resource sharing programs will evolve and the transition steps to move toward the vision described above. Requirements for restructured resource sharing are large investment in network infrastructure, information appliances, information content, and a policy framework for continued development and expansion. Achieving the vision of user-centered, ubiquitous information access and delivery services will be neither simple nor direct. At the most fundamental level, there is a divergence between the vision of universal electronic access and the as yet incomplete physical, organizational, and policy structures. While some of the basic architectural components of the new electronic scholarly access system are in place, there is a need for accelerating the completion of the electronic system infrastructure to support the demands of users for access to and delivery of distributed information. Reliable network access will at a minimum include electronic mail, fax, remote login, database browsing, digital document storage, and financial transaction services. An essential requirement is the need to scale up the information management architecture to support hundreds of thousands of users and to store multi-gigabyte databases. Additional navigation and retrieval tools capable of identifying, accessing, and retrieving the digital resources must also be developed.

It is understandable that the current emphasis is on the opportunities offered by information technologies. While there is a fundamental discontinuity in the shift to delivery of content instead of the physical item, much can be gained by drawing on the lessons of the past to identify the critical success factors for restructuring resource sharing programs in the electronic environment. Three preconditions are: online bibliographic access; efficient and rapid delivery of materials; and strong collections of research materials distributed at multiple sites. The recent article by Patricia Dominguez and Luke Swindler highlights key principles underlying effective resource sharing:[10]

- Circumstances must be conducive to cooperation.
- Most cooperative efforts have involved only research materials. Undergraduate and heavily used graduate titles, basic texts, core serials and other high demand materials have been excluded.
- Shared leadership with participating libraries taking an active role in determining policies and activities.
- Balance between local priorities and institutional self-interest and the "common good."

- Recognizing the critical role of the human resources component. Effective cooperation must build on a partnership and close cooperation among subject or area specialists. Faculty, students and other users must also be partners in the cooperative enterprise.

For all resource sharing programs, there is a need to articulate service policies and performance standards and to maintain the institutional arrangements and commitments. Finally there is a need for agreements on financial arrangements and for oversight and management.

These will be essential characteristics in the future. Indeed many of the questions, which past cooperative collection management efforts grappled with, remain, namely: coordination problems, technical impediments, human resource and political issues. Technology will solve some problems in resource sharing, but it will engender others. It is also critical to recognize that greater reliance on electronic resource sharing will not replace resource sharing of the vast holdings of existing print resources. While availability of digitized resources will accelerate, libraries will still have to manage hybrid systems that will require improvements in the present interlibrary lending and borrowing services.

CONCLUSION

Resource sharing in the electronic environment will fundamentally change how libraries operate internally and externally. For users, the promise of gaining timely, effective access to the vast but distributed research resources in North America is a powerful force for changing their patterns of information use. Continuing concerns will be how to fund the costs of networked information. Taking full advantage of shared electronic resources requires substantial investments in the network infrastructure, equipment acquisition and maintenance, staffing, and training. These and other problems will not be easy to resolve, but information technology is a powerful catalyst for improved resource sharing among libraries in an ever-widening circle of libraries.

NOTES

1. Martha Kyrillidou and Kendon Stubbs, "Supply and Demand in ARL Libraries," *ARL*, 175 (July 1994): 4.

2. Ibid.

3. *Realizing the Information Future: The Internet and Beyond* (Washington, D.C., National Academy Press, 1994): 17.

4. Anthony M. Cummings et al. *University Libraries and Scholarly Communication: A Study Prepared for The Andrew W. Mellon Foundation.* (Washington, D.C.: Association of Research Libraries, 1992) 161.

5. Ibid.

6. *Realizing the Information Future: 138.*

7. Ibid.

8. Association of American Universities Research Libraries Project: *Reports of the AAU Task Forces.* (Washington, D.C.: Association of Research Libraries, 1994), 13.

9. CIC Strategic Planning Initiative. Unpublished manuscript, 1994. [p. 2].

10. Patricia Buck Domingues and Luke Swindler, "Cooperative Collection Development at the Triangle Research University Libraries: A Model for the Nation," *College & Research Libraries* (November 1993): 470-496.

Resource Sharing and Prices

Malcolm Getz

Some informed participants in the discussion about how to use electronic systems to distribute information suggest that introduction of prices will "stultify" scholarship. Others note that introduction of prices in other sectors of our society liberated consumers, giving them many more choices at lower costs than are found when prices are not used. Some observers are unwilling to see libraries, who are significant net lenders to other libraries, be compensated for their services, arguing that information should be a "public good" and so should always be fully subsidized. Others sense that if flows among libraries are to become substantial, then net providers require financial incentives to make their resources available. Some activists promote a user-powered regime to encourage library clients to scan the Internet for information products and initiate requests for themselves. There is disagreement, however. Will clients be confused by layering prices for alternatives on top of what already appears to be a bewildering array of choices for electronic access? Or will clients be empowered by facing bona fide prices for specific services and so be better able to make informed choices?

The role of prices for information is controversial, whether between libraries, or more especially, to library clients. This essay discusses resource sharing broadly so as to identify the relationship between price, cost, and the well-being of consumers of information.

Malcolm Getz is a faculty member in the Department of Economics and Business Administration at Vanderbilt University in Nashville, TN.

[Haworth co-indexing entry note]: "Resource Sharing and Prices." Getz, Malcolm. Co-published simultaneously in *Journal of Library Administration* (The Haworth Press, Inc.) Vol. 21, No. 1/2, 1995, pp. 77-108; and *The Future of Resource Sharing* (ed: Shirley K. Baker, and Mary E. Jackson) The Haworth Press, Inc., 1995, pp. 77-108. Multiple copies of this article/chapter may be purchased from The Haworth Document Delivery Center [1-800-342-9678; 9:00 a.m. - 5:00 p.m. (EST)].

© 1995 by The Haworth Press, Inc. All rights reserved.

MECHANISMS

In broad terms, societies have four mechanisms for sharing resources and these mechanisms are as applicable to the sharing of information resources among libraries and their patrons as to other social purposes. As new technologies create new opportunities for sharing, the mix of sharing mechanisms may change. An understanding of how relative costs may change with new technologies should be useful in redesigning library programs for sharing information. The changes afoot are quite deep and so the discussion must go to fundamentals.

The first two mechanisms for resource sharing involve voluntary exchange. A person makes a judgment about contributing resources to the social pool, weighing the personal value of the resources given to the pool against the value of the resources the person takes from the pool in exchange. If the resources received are more valued than the resources contributed, the person will be made better off by participating in the exchange. Generally, such exchanges occur through individual transactions between willing parties. Because both parties in each exchange must be better off when a voluntary exchange occurs, we may infer that the society is enriched by all such exchanges.

One might think that the resources to be withdrawn from the pool must equal, in the aggregate, the resources contributed to the pool. When the total of the contributions (positives) add out with total withdrawals (negatives), the situation is a zero sum game. If the total withdrawals are less than the total contributions, as is typically true in a lottery, the situation is a negative sum game. Fortunately, in most social exchanges, the total value of withdrawals from the social pool far exceeds the value of the total contributions. When the fact of the exchange increases the value of the resources, sharing is a positive sum game. Economic progress over the centuries derives in large measure from the fact that the gains from resource sharing broadly defined have continued to increase. Adam Smith wrote about the gains from the division of labor; such gains derive from resource sharing. In thinking about the new possibilities for resource sharing among libraries and readers, one may hope to find ways to design the institutions for sharing so that the yield from sharing, the net benefits, are as large as possible.

Barter

One mechanism for resource sharing involves voluntary exchanges in-kind. People may barter for personal services and home-grown foodstuffs. Libraries sometimes view their interlibrary transactions as collective barter arrangements. They may decide how many items to lend per year so as to maintain some balance with the number of items they will borrow. Or they may track historical borrowing patterns and seek to maintain prospective parity on a bilateral basis. They typically give favorable consideration to requests from libraries from which they often borrow and less-favorable consideration to requests from libraries who give poor lending service. Barter regimes fill with complexity as increasing demands are made on them.

Barter, then, has a natural limit as a mechanism for resource sharing. The more demands placed on the system, the more cumbersome the mechanism and the poorer the performance. Moreover, the system depends on the ethical behavior of participants. The system is not to be abused—items loaned are returned or made good. Excessive demands are not to be made on the system.

Monetary Exchange

A second mechanism for resource sharing involves voluntary exchange for money. Each transaction bears a price in money. Each participant decides whether a particular transaction is worthwhile by weighing the value of the resource to be shared against its stated price. In devising interlibrary loan regimes, many libraries have sought to avoid the expense of submitting invoices for each transaction and so view barter as less expensive. However, electronics should markedly lower the costs of making transactions and so allow monetary exchange to play new roles.

The gains to readers of the voluntary exchange can be substantial. To cite Benjamin Franklin's idea, if 100 people contribute the funds each would have committed to enhancement of his or her personal library, say the cost of adding 100 volumes, they might share a library of 10,000 volumes. Access to a much larger, and so more varied collection, should improve the readers' well-being substantially. Of course, the resources sufficient to add 100 volumes to

THE FUTURE OF RESOURCE SHARING

a personal collection yield fewer titles in a library. The library requires dedicated space, a more substantial catalog or other finding system, and staff resources to manage the enterprise. Perhaps the shared library will have only 3,000 to 4,000 volumes. In addition, the library is less convenient, with limited hours, some distance from each home. Nevertheless, the library is likely to be more than an order of magnitude better than the equivalent effort devoted to additions to multiple personal libraries. The gains from resource sharing, then, may be substantial. Note that Franklin financed his library by subscription, including annual fees.

An advantage of monetary exchange is that each claimant can reveal how much value he or she places on a specific transaction. Is delivery within a day worth the extra cost? Is a photocopy to mark-up worth its cost? Is examination of the last two or three items on a long list on a topic worth the cost? When the incremental cost of a dimension of service like photocopying is obvious and direct, libraries tend to impose incremental charges and invite users to reveal whether the extra service is worth the cost. If no charge is imposed, say for photocopies, users will treat the service as though its cost is zero. Suppose the price for photocopies is set to zero even though the cost of paper, toner, and machine wear is four cents per copy. Readers will make many more photocopies than they would make were the price set at four cents. These extra copies have a value to readers less than the four cents (else they would have made them when the price was four cents) but the cost of producing the copies is still four cents for each. The difference in the values the readers place on the extra copies (less than four cents) and the cost of each copy (four cents) is a reduction in the benefits derived from resource sharing. To this extent, resource sharing with photocopies priced at zero works like a negative sum game. This situation may arise whenever the incremental gain to users in making a withdrawal from the social pool of resources is less than the value of the resources used to provide the specific service. In this case, resource sharing has negative consequences.

The unique advantage of using prices, then, is the subtlety with which individuals can reveal their preferences for particular dimensions of a service. Without prices, it is difficult for users to identify relative urgency and the importance of image quality, to signal such values to libraries, and for libraries to signal to one another, that one transaction is worth the cost of overnight delivery while for another, the lower cost of a ten day postal delivery is the best choice. When the transactions are monetized, these signals are easier.

Grants

A third mechanism for resource sharing depends on grants rather than direct exchange. The activity of giving may be based on ritual, familial relationships, a sense of community, or very broad humanitarian principles. Individuals contribute to the social pool on the basis of their status and consume from the pool on the same basis. In the case of a potlatch, the rules for giving and getting, often wrapped in ritual or long tradition, assure that the rich take less than they contribute, and the poor take more than they contribute. In the case of direct philanthropy, the giver may gain status or satisfaction from the act of giving, a sense of sustaining the human family. Interlibrary loan flows in some cases have the qualities of the potlatch, such that the more able institutions contribute more than they receive and the have-nots receive more than they contribute.

The grant mechanism will be stronger the shorter the social distance between the giver and the beneficiary. Grants work best within families or small communities. Grants to strangers require a more abstract altruism, and are subject to doubts about the consequences. Is the street urchin Fagin's agent? Is the distant, needy library poorly managed? Are its sponsors shirking their responsibilities?

The grant mechanism also affords the recipient of service little opportunity to reveal preferences for dimensions of service. A library may limit its service to a standard level: items lent without charge, but with a ten-day turn around and never a photocopy. The notion is that the truly needy won't mind the poor service. When the quality of service matters as in medical care, grant-based research, or time-bound instructional programs, grant-based service may be unsatisfactory.

Taxes

A fourth mechanism of resource sharing is that of command, wherein the taxing authority of government takes resources from

THE FUTURE OF RESOURCE SHARING

some and uses them as the government decides. It may either give the resources directly to others as with social security or use the resources to provide services, for example, roads or the national defense. Many libraries are financed in part by taxes and so make resources available by rules defined by the taxing authority. For example, each government may define rules for interlibrary flows for those libraries it finances. The governing board of a flagship state university may, then, set rules so that its library lends materials to any citizen of the state. Similarly, a local public library board may decide to offer service gratis only to residents of the municipality.

Taxation has appeal as a mechanism for resource sharing when the other mechanisms are seriously flawed. For example, voluntary monetary exchange works well for products for which the whole benefit of the product accrues to the purchaser, and only the purchaser, as with food. In such cases, the price of the product carries full information about the claim on resources made in the exchange. In contrast, when the consumption of the product has non-monetary consequences beyond the immediate participants in the transaction, its price may carry misleading information. If listening to loud music inconveniences a concert's neighbors, then the price of the concert ticket does not represent the full "cost" of the performance. The ticket price is too low and too many such performances will occur if revenue from ticket sales is the only determinant of the number of performances. (Zoning or noise abatement regulations respond to the problem.)

In an extreme case, there may be little or no possibility of exchange for a particular product or service. If one person consumes and many others benefit without paying, then there may be little or no possibility of exchange. Consider national defense or even the maintenance of a prominent landmark like the Lincoln Memorial. Each of us may value the service in a significant way. However, if asked to contribute financially in proportion to the value we place on the service, we may suspect that others will contribute. So, it will pay each of us individually to say that we value the service not at all and so escape making payment. Given the chance, each of us will behave as a free rider, enjoying the service while paying nothing. When each consumer has an incentive to disguise his or her true preferences, then voluntary exchange is unlikely to yield a high level of gain from resource sharing. Keeping out agricultural pests, vaccinating people for communicable diseases, restraining the level of ocean fishing (no one pays to retain breeding stocks), even limiting deforestation (no one pays for the forest's value in flood control or the oxygen the forests provide) reflect significant free rider problems.

Markets may fail for other reasons as well and so the philosophical basis for taxation, government spending, and regulation is broad. Markets with monopolies or excessive market power may justify government regulation or provision of services. An excessive concentration of income, wealth, and authority in the hands of a few as well as the well-being of the least well off may justify various government policies. Voluntary exchange through markets is a valuable social invention, but it is seldom perfect.

Even in those cases where voluntary exchange is obviously flawed, the problem of deciding on a level of service remains. With dependence on taxation comes reliance on a political process for decisions about organization and service levels. The political process may reflect the wishes of the median voter, or the result of coalition building, or the influences of organized interests who are willing to help finance campaigns or solicit voters. The political process may have its own flaws and so limit the gains from resource sharing by taxation. The process by which the ocean fisheries of the world have been depleted was well understood during the several decades when it occurred. Still, governments were unable to take corrective action.

Libraries can and do limit services to specific clients and exclude others. The benefits of using library materials accrue immediately to the persons who have access. Serving additional persons typically involves some incremental costs, particularly in the electronic arena where costs may be linked to the number of simultaneous users. Thus, just as bookstores make information products available to their clients for fees, so may libraries. To argue that a library is sufficiently distinct from a bookstore in distributing information and offering services so as to justify taxation finance and exposure to the political process, one will need some careful reasoning. To what extent does the library serve disadvantaged persons or educational functions? To what extent does the use of the library serve

84 THE FUTURE OF RESOURCE SHARING

citizenship functions? Who bears the burden of the taxes to pay for the library? Why is a subsidy to the library more appropriate than a subsidy to a bookstore?

Mixed Mechanisms

These four mechanisms for resource sharing are present in every modern society. Each is advantageous in particular circumstances. Yet, each has problems that limit its appeal. In designing resource sharing·mechanisms in a specific circumstance, a society will face trade offs among several objectives. Barter is suitable for low levels of exchange and often has some of the feel of a grant. Pricing mechanisms are often, but not always, best at getting the maximum gain from sharing resources. Grants are often best at building communities and providing for disadvantaged groups. Taxation is essential for achieving broad social purposes, but is confounded by the vagaries of the political process.

The four mechanisms are not mutually exclusive. Indeed, one can think of a given library exchange that reflects all four mechanisms at once as when a state university library (tax-supported) sends a copy of a journal article to a private college library with whom it has a long-standing trading relationship (barter) but charges an extra fee for fulfillment by fax (monetary transaction). The private college library lends to the state university, motivated by its philanthropic finance and its barter relationship with the university library. The mixture of mechanisms for resource sharing among libraries reflects a particular history in which interlibrary lending represented a small percentage of the use of material within a library, typically less than two percent of recorded circulations. The service provided a safety valve to meet unusual requests. The relatively low volume of activity allowed primary dependence on barter as the mechanism. Some libraries reflected philanthropic motives in filling requests for all comers. Some tax supported institutions were driven to lend by governmental authority. However, as technologies change costs for different ways of providing information, the underlying fundamentals may change in ways that may lead to quite new flows. If delivery of documents from outside the local library is to increase tenfold or more, then new institutional arrangements are likely to be necessary.

LOW COST

If resource sharing among libraries is to be a positive sum game with a growing net, the institutional arrangements should be designed carefully so as to take advantage of low-cost methods for delivering information. If given levels of services can be achieved at lower cost, the net gain from resource sharing will be larger. The core fact is that electronic document supply by network will soon be significantly less expensive than any alternative. The change in technology has a number of implications.

The cost of storing information as volumes of print on open-stack, library shelves is about $1.95 per volume per year, including the amortization of the building and shelving [Getz, 1993]. Books can be stored in compact-storage facilities at under $0.20 per volume per year, but with increased inconvenience and cost of retrieval. In contrast, texts may be stored electronically on a large scale system at under $0.04 per volume including replacement of the system on a five-year cycle and reformatting the text to new electronic devices as necessary. Note as well, the cost of electronic systems seems likely to continue to fall for many decades. The cost advantages of electronic systems are already substantial and will grow much larger.

Moreover, texts stored electronically can be delivered to a patron's worksite in a couple of minutes for modest incremental cost. The electronic storage and delivery mechanism will be both more convenient and lower in cost than storing information in print, even in compact storage. The transition from print to electronic formats will take time. Libraries need to invent systems for receiving and managing electronic texts. Publishers will need time to gain experience with producing and marketing electronic information products.

Given a document distributed as print, the cost of conversion to electronic format is substantially more than the cost of storing the print. Documents need to be distributed originally in electronic format or conversion to the electronic format must be such that the electronic format is shared among several libraries or other users for some current need. It is seldom economic for an individual library to convert print to electronic format in order to reduce its own need to store print.

Moreover, for many purposes electronic documents are more useful than print. Electronic indices, for example, allow identification of materials more quickly, more thoroughly, and more flexibly than their print counterparts. Full-text databases of poetry can be searched by individual word and so associations can be made that would be quite difficult with non-electronic methods. Databases of images of artworks, architecture, medical images, biological specimens, even catalogs of parts, are generally more useful than print, with more rapid retrieval, multiple finding paths, and built-in audio and video. Numerical information is often subjected to further analysis and graphical display—tasks that are now primarily done electronically. It is often the case, then, that electronic documents are preferred to print.

Storage vs. Communications Costs

The design of library services will depend critically on the trade off between the cost of electronic storage and the cost of data communication. If storage were very low cost, and communication off-campus were relatively expensive, including being prone to congestion and breakdown, the library would acquire electronic files, store them on campus, and make them available to users by campus network. Indeed, some files might be kept as, say, compact disks at the readers' worksites to avoid communication at the time of use.

On the other hand, if storage were relatively more expensive and communication inexpensive, then the campus would store very little and rely on the network for access to most information products. Information that is updated frequently like stock and commodity prices and news reports will be network-based regardless. Information that is seldom used anywhere, that is, archival materials, will also likely be stored once and made available to all by network because communication is infrequent. However, for the core academic literatures, those materials with long, useful lives that are used frequently, a balance will be struck between storage and communication costs. In all likelihood, substantial databases of core materials, such as all published English poetry, drama, and literary prose from a given era, will be marketed as large, pre-indexed blocks and mounted on individual major campuses so as to avoid congestion problems in communication.

For example, H. R. Haldeman's complete diaries were published in May 1994 as a compact disc with some home videos of Richard Nixon's presidency. The print version is a subset of the complete diaries and includes no video. According to Jack Gourman [1993, p. 359] there are 1,212 institutions in the U.S. offering undergraduate degree programs in history. In all likelihood, most of these will offer courses in the decades ahead that will include discussion of the 1960s and 70s; students may be invited to read the Haldeman diaries and write essays about events from that time. The Haldeman diaries could be mounted by one or a small number of organizations on the Internet with access, say, by Gopher. If suitable data communication networks become ubiquitous as many observers expect, then the students in all 1,212 history programs might use the Internet to use the Haldeman diaries. Alternatively, most of the 1,212 campuses might acquire the compact disc and mount it locally to be accessed by the campus network. Which strategy will dominate?

Technical change in data storage and in data communication are both very rapid, and a definitive answer is difficult. Materials like the Haldeman diaries that are likely to find frequent use by undergraduates for courses and essays will be acquired and mounted locally by many campuses. Storage costs will be low enough. Witness the pressure on LEXIS and Westlaw, two classic network delivery ventures. An emerging array of inexpensive CD products aimed at specialized markets allows readers to buy a CD that meets a high proportion of their needs at much less expense than, say, using LEXIS [Felsenthal, 1994]. However, for research collections, archival materials rarely used, materials updated very frequently, exhaustive collections of sharp focus are likely to be kept in only a few places with general network access dominating. If the full set of audio tapes from the Nixon White House were made available, they might be stored only in one or a few places providing general network access because the files will be voluminous and the use less frequent than the Haldeman diaries. (Excerpts of the audio might be distributed to many campuses.)

There are then powerful incentives for publishers, libraries, and readers to embrace electronic systems for distributing and using information. Electronic systems will then dominate resource sharing among libraries as they come to dominate the libraries' own core activities.

In describing the cost of storing and retrieving a given text, we are describing the cost per unit. With the continuing sharp decline in the unit cost of text in electronic formats, we may expect a significant, continuing growth in the use of all information products. The total budget for information services may change little as the decline in unit costs is offset to a substantial degree by the increase in the quantity of information used.

USAGE PATTERNS

Making these ideas more formal yields some additional insight. Suppose that the cost of storing print in open shelves with 36 inch aisles is $1.95 per volume per year [Getz, 1993]. If an average volume costs $44 to acquire and $27 to process, the library has an up front cost of $71 per volume [Carpenter and Getz, 1994]. However, usage of most volumes occurs in the first years after its acquisition. If ninety percent of the uses that ever occur come in the first decade of acquisition, then most of the cost of acquisition should be assigned to those years of high use. Once a typical volume reaches an age of say ten years or so, it is reasonable to assume that the cost of acquisition is a sunk cost and so to focus only on the carrying costs, namely, the cost of storage and the cost of retrieval. Suppose that retrieval from open stacks requires the user to commit time worth about $4 and that the library incurs cost of $1 in circulating and reshelving materials, on average, for each retrieval. The following expression gives the total cost to the library of storage and retrieval activity for a year for one volume, given the number of times, R, that it is retrieved.

(1)   Open Stack Cost per year $= \$1.95 + \quad \$5 * R$

The use of an on-site, compact storage facility with robotic retrieval may involve an annual cost per volume of $0.84 for storage and about $2 of library cost and $6 of user time and delay cost in retrieval.

(2)   Robotic Stack per year   = $0.84 + $8 * R

A remote compact storage facility might cost $0.20 per year per volume for storage. Retrieval may cost the library $6, and the user may incur time and delay costs worth $10, for a total cost of retrieval of $16.

(3)   Remote Storage Cost per year   = $0.20 + $16 * R

Borrowing from a remote library or other service provider with conventional costs might be $29 per transaction [Research Libraries Group/Association of Research Libraries, 1993]. This figure is the cost of the typical borrowing library in placing a request through conventional interlibrary loan, about $19, plus the cost of the typical lending library of filling a request, about $11. Add to the libraries' costs a cost to the reader of the inconvenience and delay in getting supply from an external source of $15 (say). The total cost of external supply might then be about $44 per fulfillment.

(4)   External Supply per year   = $44 * R

Figure 1 shows the total cost of storage plus retrieval in annual per volume terms for a range of rates of retrieval for these four methods of fulfilling user demands when acquisition costs are viewed as sunk. For volumes used more than 0.37 times per year (that is, about once in three years), storage on open-stack shelves will give the lowest total cost. For items used more than the 0.08 but less than 0.37 times per year (that is, once in 3 to 12 years), the on-site, compact storage with robotic retrieval is least cost. For items used between 0.08 and 0.007 times per year (that is, between once in 13 and 135 years), the remote compact storage facility will have lowest cost. For items used less than 0.007 times per year (less than once in 135 years), the conventional interlibrary loan service or other external supply offers lowest cost. Figure 1 shows the major choices available to libraries in the early 1990s in a stylized fashion. Note, again, that this analysis assumes that the libraries have acquired the materials for an earlier purpose that represents a sunk cost.

FIGURE 1. Costs of Storage and Retrieval

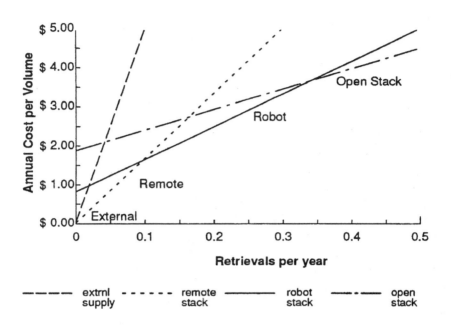

Electronic Systems

Extending the analysis to emerging electronic systems for storing and delivering information shows a dramatic shift. The cost of storing information in electronic format is about $0.04 per year, given that the information comes to the library in electronic format and that the acquisition costs are fully amortized in the early years of ownership. (This figure assumes a five year service life on a tape-cartridge electronic storage system.) Retrieval might cost the library $0.50 in computer systems (assuming a five year service life on a computer of substantial scale with a considerable volume of activity) and the time and other cost of the reader might be $2.00. (The notion is that the reader devotes some time to locating and retrieving an item by network. If the services of the local network are charged per use, there may some network fee included here. This figure is speculative.)

(5)   Local Electronic Storage Cost per year   = $0.04 + $2.50 R

Similarly, information products might be ordered and delivered from remote sites by network. Suppose that network services evolve to the point where transactions may be readily accounted for and so the cost of completing individual transactions is quite low. Suppose the cost of network delivery is $1 per item delivered and the time and other cost to the reader is identical to that from a campus electronic depository.

(6)   Network Delivery per year   = $3.00 R

The cost of the two electronic modes of delivery are summarized in Figure 2. Figure 2 is a magnification of the lower, left-corner of Figure 1 with the two electronic modes added. The two lines representing the electronic modes are deliberately made thick to suggest that the relationships represent speculation about future possibilities. Although the costs of the electronic modes will lie sharply below the conventional modes shown in Figure 1, the exact position will continue to change over time as the position of the electronic modes will continue to fall downward and to the right. The specific relationships shown here as representative of future possibilities suggest that items used less frequently than 0.08 times per year (once in 12.5 years) will have lowest cost from the remote network service. For all higher levels of usage, local campus storage in electronic format with campus network delivery dominates.

Of course, the differential in the cost of delivery from a campus-based system and a remote network system plays a pivotal role. If the remote service were as reliable, convenient, and low cost in delivery as the campus-based service, then network delivery might wholly dominate. In addition, the cost for local electronic storage assumes that the campus stores electronic items on a considerable scale and captures most of the available advantages of scale in electronic storage. Small campuses will face higher storage costs and so tend to make greater use of network delivery.

Local storage has several advantages. First, the national network is inherently subject to congestion as long as it does not bear prices related to use. Although some observers believe that the invention and deployment of ever faster communications technologies will

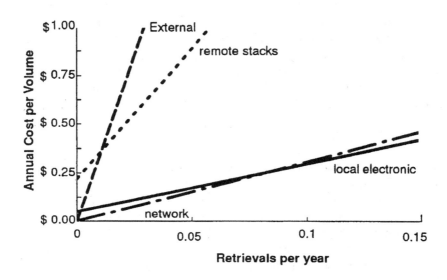

FIGURE 2. Cost of Electronic Systems

keep ahead of demand, in fact, congestion has been a common occurrence on the Internet. (Without prices, the Internet may face a future like that of citizen's band radio: congestion and abuse may make it highly undesirable.) In addition, as more documents containing multimedia elements move over the network, the demand for bandwidth will escalate very rapidly. In the end, congestion is likely to be mitigated only by the introduction of prices. As commercial ventures seek to deliver video on demand to residences and elsewhere, network services beyond the campus are likely to bear prices. If network service beyond the campus bears prices related to the volume of use, then the campus-based storage of commonly used materials will continue to have an important role. If the off-campus network service remains unpriced, it will be likely to give such poor service as to be unreliable, and campus storage will be even more important.

Second, some vendors of information services may wish to license their products for unlimited, campus-wide use. They may expect to sell such "subscriptions" to each campus, much as they sell subscriptions to campus libraries today. The campus-wide license would allow faculty and staff to make whatever copies they like, whether print or electronic, integrate materials into packages for sale to students, and use in electronic bulletin boards, as long as access is limited to persons affiliated with the campus. A number of software vendors already offer campus-wide licenses. Some vendors of video tapes sell a license for private, non-commercial use that allows use in class and on campus systems as long as the material isn't resold. Some non-profit publishers are considering granting such "campus" rights to their print publications by printing an appropriate authorization in each issue. Such rights should allow the publisher to avoid the cost of responding to multiple individual requests for permission to copy, yet retain the copyright in such a fashion as to assure sales revenues from each campus. In some sense, the campus-wide license to copy might justify the higher rates typically charged to libraries. As campus-wide licenses become common, the campus-based storage system may retain an advantage over remote, network suppliers.

Cooperative Buying

The analysis changes when materials are purchased to be shared. The buyers' cooperative, wherein one organization acquires material for use by many, means that the cost of acquiring and processing materials must be included in the analysis and so will likely be reflected in prices when prices are used. The organization might be a library's library like the Center for Research Libraries. It might be a for-profit venture like Engineering Information. The responsibility for acquisition might be distributed among cooperating libraries along the lines of the Farmington plan. The essential feature of the buyers' cooperative is that the institution doing the buying acquires materials for collective use that it would not otherwise have acquired. The acquiring organization must then have sufficient revenue to support its extra acquisitions program. Unless there is some external source of funding, the revenue stream must come from the participants in the cooperative. The revenues might be in the form of annual membership by libraries as with the Center for Research Libraries, an annual subscription fee to individual users, or in the form of pay per use as with Engineering Information. The prices when they are used–whether annual subscriptions or pay per use–will be at levels that reflect the amortization of the full cost of doing business, ordering, paying for, cataloging, storing, and delivering items.

Suppose that the cost of acquiring a volume is $44 and the cost of processing and storing it is $27, for a total upfront cost of $71.[1] Operation of a cooperative adds administrative overhead in coordination and governance, say, of $27 per volume. Assume that the cooperative stores its items in remote facilities at $2. The total cost of acquisition, storage, and overhead might then be $100 per volume. Assume, as in equation 4, that delivery costs $43. In this analysis, the costs are viewed as incurred once for all time.

For the buying cooperative, one might assume that the acquisition cost is incurred once for the group, and split among the members of the cooperative. For simplicity, here there are taken to be 20 members of the cooperative who are equally likely to use each item. The relationship between retrievals and cost per volume when acquisition costs are taken into account is shown in Figure 3. The $100 cost is divided by 20 for the external supply by the cooperative arrangement. Note that the cost structure provides for the delivery of physical items, so issues of copyright do not arise. All the local storage options shown in Figure 1 are recast in Figure 3 to include the $100 cooperative acquisition cost.[2]

When one takes explicit account of the cost of acquisition, the buying cooperative is attractive for low use material. Given the assumptions here, the buying cooperative lowers total cost for items used less than 2.14 times. For items expected to be used more than 2.14 times and less than 3.33, robotic retrieval offers the least cost. Open stacks give least cost for items used more than 3.33 times. Remote storage dedicated to a single library is dominated by the buying cooperative using remote storage. Even if the buying cooperative has only two members, the cooperative will offer lower total costs for items expected to be used less than 0.86 times.

The possibility of cooperative buying with electronic tools is more difficult to analyze because it involves speculation about how markets will evolve in a rapidly changing technological arena. We may suppose that the campus library may acquire electronic materials and store them. To be concrete, suppose that acquisitions costs

FIGURE 3. Total Cost per Volume with Acquisition Costs

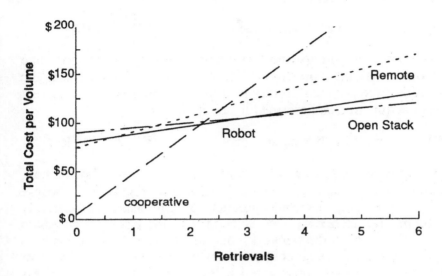

are similar to those incurred for comparable print volumes. Although many early electronic products come at premium prices, over time competition may reduce their price. If electronic products come in large bundles, the library's processing costs may be reduced. On the tentative assumption that acquisition costs remain about the same, then the cost of local electronic storage including acquisition, processing, and storage will be given by equation (5').

(5') Local Electronic Storage with Acquisition = $71.40 + $2.50 R

The assumption here is that publishers will find their profits maximized by licensing their electronic products for use on one campus for about the current price plus processing cost in the library.

The remaining possibility is that readers use the national network to access electronic materials when license fees for network access are included in the cost structure. One must speculate about what level of license fees will obtain. Toward the high end, one might imagine fees at levels comparable to what a library would pay to license the electronic products for mounting on the campus network. Call this "network access with local license." Such costs are described in equation 6'.

(6')   Network with Local License   = \$71 + \$3 R

Alternatively, perhaps the level of license fee will be more like that of the buying cooperative for print materials, such that the acquisition fee per local library is, say, one twentieth of the current cost of acquisition as described in equation 6".

(6")   Network with Shared License   = \$71/20 + \$3 R

In Figure 4, these three electronic cost patterns overlay the conventional cost structures previously shown in Figure 3. If license fees for mounting electronic products on campuses are relatively low compared to license fees embedded in the prices of access to services remote on the network, then local mounting will have an important role. Buying cooperatives that depend on delivery of electronic copies of copyrighted materials will be useful for less frequently used materials. On the assumptions here, items with an expected usage greater than 0.80 would be mounted locally. The cost of the seldom used items accessed by network is comparable to that of a buying cooperative holding a single print copy of the item. At the other extreme, if the copyright license fees for use of materials over the network are below those for mounting the products on campus, then remote access will dominate for all but quite frequently used items.

The two important unknowns are first, the price structure and communications services available on the national network and, second, the level of copyright license fees for campus mounting versus remote use on the national network. The issue of price levels is addressed more fully below.

USER POWER

The net gain from resource sharing can also be increased by assuring that the claims on resources are those that will have the highest value to consumers of information. In general, the value of

FIGURE 4. Total Cost per Volume with Acquisition Cost and Electronic Systems

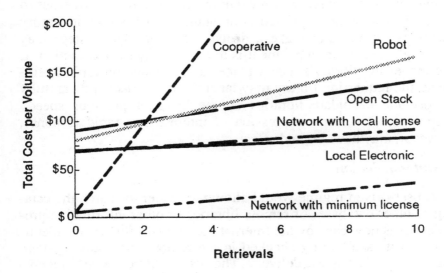

the service can be made as large as possible by tailoring each transaction carefully to each user. Because users know their own interests best, empowering users to make claims for specific services is likely to yield the most valuable services. That is, users can decide whether faster service, more units of service, higher resolution, and more care in undertaking exhaustive searches are worth the cost. Users can be entrusted with the authority to make such choices on each transaction only if they carry the responsibility of living within budgets and are informed by and react to suitable prices.

Conventional interlibrary loan operations typically have required the reader to fill out a written form requesting an item. A library staff member captures information from the request form, verifies the accuracy of the description of the item, checks to see whether the local library holds the item, and then seeks to identify an external source and some alternatives. In identifying sources, the staff member will weigh the likelihood that the candidate source will respond in a timely manner, whether too many or too few requests have to be placed to each source given the number of items lent to each or other traditional or contractual associations. A staff member at the candidate source will receive the request, decide whether to act on it, verify the requested item against that library's inventory (catalog) system, and make a decision to lend. These steps may occur whether or not a payment is to accompany the transaction. If the requesting library's reader places a high value on rapid fulfillment, the requesting library may label the order *rush* and carefully choose the candidate libraries on the basis of previous speedy responses. The user's expression of interest in a rapid response, however, may have limited effect.

Disintermediation

A user-driven regime would allow the reader to search the catalog or other databases of remote libraries or other information providers as is now easy by the Internet. Once a specific item is identified and its availability checked in the remote circulation system, the user might request delivery. The distant library would receive the request on its own system, already checked against its inventory. It's system might print a mailing label (or give a fax number or electronic address) so that a student worker with little training could fill the request. This process stream has the user selecting the source and doing the verification against the supplier's database with substantially lower costs than the conventional, staff-intensive process. If one thinks of the conventional process as being intermediated by the library, then making the process user-centered involves disintermediation.

The disintermediation should allow deliveries to be requested and filled at dramatically lower cost than with intermediation. The user will naturally perform many of the steps now performed by library staff. In the conventional process, the borrowing library incurs about $19 worth of cost per request, mostly in staff time [Research Library Group/Association of Research Libraries, 1993]. With total disintermediation, this cost might drop to near zero for many transactions. The lending library now incurs about $11 of cost to fill a request, but some of that cost involves staff time in data entry and checking. Perhaps this cost will be reduced as well. The cost per transaction might drop to well under $10 for items that users request directly from remote libraries and other suppliers. The borrower's library will get notice of the transaction, retain responsibility for making payments, and tracking overdues.

If readers are to have the authority to make extensive demands on remote suppliers, then they must also have commensurate responsibility. If delivery from external sources is to increase tenfold in a typical academic library, then the resources devoted to such flows will be substantial. The demands on suppliers will be great and should be carefully managed. If such services are to yield information services of high value, then readers must have incentives to use the service responsibly.

When the remote services involve specific costs for each transaction, then users need to understand the cost of each transaction before requesting service. When a service is unpriced, users will naturally use it even when the value generated is less than the cost of providing the service, as with unpriced photocopies. When an array of services is priced, users will reflect on the value of each claim for service, and request service only when the value is expected to exceed the cost. With different sources bearing different prices, readers will weigh cost against differences in the quality of services. Indeed, readers will decide about the method, timeliness, and quality of delivery, weighing alternatives in each instance against its cost. In this way, users will reveal which dimensions of service are worth the cost in each instance, and so extract the most valuable set of information services from the resources at hand.

Integration of Disparate Services

Putting budgets and prices directly in the hands of readers has the further advantage of allowing the easy integration of a variety of suppliers. Any library with a catalog on the Internet is a possible supplier. Those whose catalogs are compliant with the Z39.50 standard for communication are likely to be used more readily [for example, Fedunok and Bonk, 1994]. Those who support the emerging Z39.63 standard for communication regarding requests for delivery should be particularly successful in attracting requests for service. Those who engender a reputation for speedy, reliable response will attract more requests. Some libraries may generate a significant income from filling requests for delivery. The cost of managing the flow of funds should be kept low by reliance on the transfer of electronic funds through a central repository. OCLC has launched a reimbursement system for interlibrary loan that will play a role.

Other information suppliers will play a role as well. For example, Engineering Information, Inc. delivers articles on demand for a fee. With a database readily available to the Internet linked to an electronic funds system, EI should be able to offer very competitive services. UnCover, UMI's campus-based page image service, and a variety of other information products and services should play together on the campus network in a fashion that allows users to get delivery of a significant body of literature in a timely manner on demand.

Academic institutions are likely to want to subsidize access to information for their clients. In effect, the print library subsidizes information by using budgeted funds to acquire and store materials. For its clients, the library subsidizes the information it acquires. The client must still arrange a trip to the library to identify and fetch the materials. With user initiated requests and delivery directly to users on demand, the subsidy will likely be more explicit. A college may establish an account with a grant of funds for each reader to use in acquiring information. With limited funds and bona fide prices, users will choose carefully how, when, and what information products to use. The library will offer guidance in use, troubleshoot when service fails, and continue to intermediate requests for unusual materials. A principal way to empower users is to establish accounts and allow users to respond to prices.

With the ready accessibility of a significant quantity of valuable information products for delivery on demand by network, libraries may face the anomalous situation of having service from remote sources by network be more convenient than books in its own stacks. That is, network oriented services will deliver documents directly to readers on demand for fees. Electronic data files, full-text or otherwise, may often be directly accessible whether stored on the campus or remotely. For articles, the delivery may be by fax. For books, remote libraries may ship volumes directly to users by overnight service for appropriate fees. For readers who value convenience, the fee-based network delivery may be quite popular, particularly when the network providers offer more comprehensive collections than the local library. To compete, the library will likely want to offer convenient delivery from its own collections for a fee. In this way, the various delivery options may be well integrated, and the library's investments in collections may continue to play a front-line role.

A library that opts not to allow its users to see the costs of individual elements of service through prices will suffer several handicaps. First, as the demand for delivery of products by network grows, the library will face the challenge of rationing access so as to continue to live within its budgets. If network delivery proves popular, the claim on library resources will grow. The library will seek ways to assure that the claims on remote services are legitimate and highly valued. It may devote staff resources to monitoring requests to assure that the resources are not available locally, that the requester is of appropriate status, perhaps even to assure that the request is well formulated. Such intermediation adds cost. Second, the library may face the difficulty that network delivery is more convenient than meeting demands from its own collection. Even if using materials in the library's own collection is less expensive than use of a remote service, library users may seek the higher quality, network-based service when it is presented as free. Third, the library will be faced with multiple sources of supply for the same kinds of documents, with different sources offering different prices and qualities of service. Will this user value the extra cost, faster service of supplier X or will the lower cost, slower service from supplier Y suffice? When the readers see the prices and gain experience with different suppliers, they may reveal their preferences. The library may be of counsel. If the library staff do not know how users value different dimensions of service in each instance, the library may opt to save money, and so offer consistently poor service. Or it may opt for rapid supply, but at a higher cost. In either case, the net benefits of resource sharing are not as high as they could be were each reader able to reveal his or her preference in each case.

PRICES

The careful reader will note that the case made for prices for network delivery of information services here is not one of generating revenues. Bartering, granting, and taxing generate revenues.

Prices here are not advanced primarily as a method of passing along costs. Market prices often depart widely from costs. Indeed, in the market place for academic journals, prices from for-profit publishers often are triple those from non-profit publishers for journals of comparable frequency, page count, and citation impact [Carpenter and Getz, 1994]. Price, then, may reflect the market power of the seller (or in some cases, the buyer).

Market power is the ability of the seller to raise price without losing too many sales. In formal terms, one might measure the percentage change in quantity sold as a ratio to a given percentage increase in price. If a seller raises price a little and suffers a large percentage decrease in sales, the seller has little market power. The price elasticity of the demand to the firm is high. In this case, the firm is in a relatively competitive market and prices will be close to costs. If a seller raises price and suffers little percentage loss in sales, the seller has much more market power. The demand to the firm is relatively price inelastic. In this case, the firm will tend to set price well above cost [Watson and Getz, 1981, pp. 329-52]. The market power of the firm, the ability to raise price with modest loss of sales, is an important influence in the market for scholarly information products.

With libraries as intermediaries, for-profit scholarly publishers have discovered that their demand curves have low price elasticity. They are able to raise prices substantially with modest loss of sales. They have significant market power and exploit it by moving prices to levels several multiples over incremental cost. Libraries make decisions to drop journal titles only reluctantly and with delays.

As long as many journals come from for-profit publishers and exhibit demands with low price elasticities, we may expect the prices to be quite high. A shift to electronic distribution will be unlikely to change such pricing policies, as long as the elasticities of demand remain low.

However, with electronic delivery, the nature of the market might change. Shifting the distribution system to one that is user powered, with users able to seek individual items with payments made with each transaction, may yield demands for information products that are substantially more elastic with respect to price. That is, the quantity of information products purchased by users may be quite sensitive to price. In undertaking a significant project, a user may make a decision about whether looking at ten more articles will be worthwhile. If the price is 15 cents per page, the user may respond differently than if the price is $1.50 per page. The difference in response rate means that demand will be more price elastic, therefore, profit maximizing prices will be closer to costs. (To give an example from another industry, note that MacDonald's maximizes its profit by responding to very price elastic demands for fast food by offering low prices.)

Moreover, publishers typically practice price discrimination. They know that the demand for journals from individuals is much more elastic than the demand from libraries. As a result, they seek to segment their markets, and charge more to libraries than to individuals. In a user-powered market place with prices playing an intermediating role, price discrimination against libraries may be more difficult. After all, it is the user who is to make the spending decision.

Even if the library subscribes to a bundle of services at an annual rate, the price for bundles may be tempered by the possibility of direct sales on the basis of individual use. That is to say, if readers have access to individual products with fees charged per use, the library will only subscribe to a bundle of service if the price on the bundle is attractive relative to the prices charged for individual transactions. If the price per use is $0.15 per page for a service where a library might expect to have 100,000 pages of use per year, then the library is unlikely to be willing to pay $15,000 per year for the subscription to avoid charges for individual use. (This assumes that the system for managing payments for transactions is electronic and works well at a fraction of a cent of cost per transaction. The library will need to gain experience and have tools that track use so as to be able to judge the cost of pay per use versus a subscription for itself.) An active market with prices charged per transaction may lower prices for information products generally.

Although publishers are likely to want to sell annual subscriptions to libraries so as to sustain the profit advantages that arise from this practice, a publisher may also wish to offer sales on a usage basis so as to generate revenues from campuses who do not subscribe and from persons not in academia. Suppose these services are by network and so, generally available to faculty and students on any campus. Suppose as well that the demand from such groups is substantial and price elastic. Then the publisher will be able to maximize profit by charging prices closer to cost because of the higher volume of sales. The license to a campus on a subscription basis, with campus-wide rights to copy, will have, as a ceiling, the cost of simply using the network service directly.

Lowering Prices

The academic world has four other gambits for dealing with high prices imposed by for-profit publishers, particularly in the scientific arenas. One is that advocated by the Association of American Universities [1994], namely to urge authors to direct their manuscripts away from publishers who charge too much and toward lower-priced journals. Universities might seek to be co-owners of their faculty's copyrights so as to play more active roles in lowering journal prices. This method of seeking to redirect manuscripts holds some promise, but faculty may be wary of foregoing their historic rights to full ownership of published works. Although they now usually assign away rights to journal articles as they are published, the publication of textbooks, literary and art works, and the like, are occasionally important alternate sources of income for faculty.

A second approach might be to encourage non-profit and society publishers to be more aggressive in launching journals at the lower prices they typically charge so as to undercut the market for highly priced journals. Some observers are particularly hopeful that new journals can be launched electronically and become successful inexpensively. If proliferation of titles is also part of the problem and if a journal title takes five to ten years to reach maturity, then this may be an expensive strategy. One might note as well that in recent decades, a number of university presses and society publishers have moved their journals to for-profit publishers.

A third approach is to appeal to the fair use doctrine in the copyright law. Under the fair use provision, an individual may make a photocopy of a part of a work for mark-up and later review, much as one might take handwritten notes as one reads. As long as one does not resell the copy or otherwise use the copy so as to undercut the market potential for the copyrighted work, readers in the U.S.

Malcolm Getz 105

are generally within the copyright law in making copies for personal use. Publishers have sought to narrow the scope of fair use, and won a suit against Texaco to prevent the corporate library from distributing photocopies of journal articles to the corporation's scientists. In conventional interlibrary loan practice, an occasional photocopy of a journal article may be sent to another library in response to a request without the permission of the copyright holder. When such copying and delivering reaches a threshold level, payment is to be made to the copyright holder, perhaps through an intermediary. The principle of fair use then has limited scope to hold down prices for journals.

As the demand for delivery of photocopies from external sites grows, it is clear that fulfillment of photocopies cannot be viewed as within the bounds of fair use. When the volume of such traffic grows, it will likely undercut the market for subscriptions and so a mechanism for making payments to copyright holders needs to be found. In a fee-based arena, collection of fees for delivery will be routine and the addition of payment to copyright holders ought to be reasonably economic. The copyright holders will, however, set the rates. If demands are relatively inelastic with respect to price, the prices may be set at relatively high levels. However, if pricing on the basis of use yields more elastic demands, then the profit-maximizing mark-ups over cost will be lower.

All in all, the prospect of pay per use in the electronic arena may be one of several changes that allow scholarly communication to occur at lower price levels.

READER WELFARE

Readers are consumers of information. Conventional libraries have served reader interests well by providing a much richer set of information resources than readers could accumulate on their own. The essence of libraries is to share information resources so that, for each reader, access to the pooled resource is significantly more valuable than using resources unpooled. Users tolerate some inconvenience in having to go to the library and deal with its formality so as to have the benefit of more diverse reading.

With electronic storage and networks, the relative costs of

106   THE FUTURE OF RESOURCE SHARING

information products are shifting so that electronic products can be delivered more conveniently and at lower expense than books in stacks. Moreover, electronic products are often preferred. As a result, readers can expect more per dollar invested from the electronic systems than they can expect from books in stacks.

The electronic arena, however, will be much larger and more diverse than a conventional library. The reader will have many more choices about where to get service. Each dimension of service may entail some difference in cost. Therefore, it is important that readers have ways to signal that a particular, more expensive dimension of service is worth the extra cost in a given instance. The best way to allow a reader to demonstrate that a specific costly service is worthwhile, is to invite the reader to respond to prices. In effect, network delivery of information products will often be more an extension of the photocopy machine than of books on the shelf.

Publishers are likely to offer campus-wide licenses for some important information products, and libraries are likely to continue to offer a significant set of services with delivery by network, often with no incremental charge. For the most part, the information resources that directly support the curriculum are likely to reside on the campus and be available without specific charges to readers.

Information that is updated frequently will come remotely via network. Important among these will likely be the working paper services and other raw materials of the scholarly process. Indeed, the working paper process that occurs on the network may support a review process that identifies the highest quality materials [Getz, "Petabytes" forthcoming]. These materials may then be packaged and distributed to subscribing campuses electronically. Similarly, the network will provide a variety of near real-time data, news, weather, satellite and remote laboratory data, and information from a variety of markets.

Seldom used materials will also likely be stored at one or only a few places and be used remotely by network as the need arises. In many instances, the suppliers will rely on prices as a source of revenues and for their role in allowing readers to signal the quality of service they prefer. More aggressive use of prices affords the ironic possibility that demands for information services will be more price elastic and so prices may be lower and closer to costs.

Most importantly, however, the cost of storing and retrieving a block of information will be significantly less in the electronic arena than in the print world. Moreover, electronic delivery should often be more convenient and the information more useful. As a consequence, we might expect significant growth in the number of blocks of information used by students, faculty, and beyond. The growth in the volume of information flow will mean that the use of external information sources may grow rapidly, even as the use of locally stored information grows. The use of electronic delivery of information will allow information to be used more frequently, for more purposes, and with greater ease. The increased use of electronic information services may be accelerated by judicious use of prices to encourage high quality service.

NOTES

1. One might think of taking explicit account of the timing of the uses. Uses typically occur over a considerable period of time in a pattern that might be described by a Poisson distribution. Because the value of future uses should be discounted to present value, they are worth less than current uses. Under plausible assumptions, however, most uses occur in the early years and with discounting at a long term real rate of interest of say three percent, the present value of expected uses may be 90 percent or more of the total expected uses that will ever occur. On this basis, as a first approximation, uses are assumed to occur early in the life of each item.

2. In the following descriptions of costs, the acquisition cost of $71 and cost of storage for each storage strategy are assumed to be expensed in year one. This illustrates the opposite extreme from ignoring acquisition costs and assuming storage and use is perpetual. A richer characterization of the timing of costs and use will require more sophisticated techniques than are appropriate here.

(1')	Open Stack	=	$90	+ $ 5	R
(2')	Robotic	=	$80	+ $ 8	R
(3')	Remote	=	$73	+ $16	R
(4')	Cooperative	=	$100/20	+ $43	R

REFERENCES

Association of American Universities. 1994. *AAU Research Libraries Project.* Washington, D.C. April 4.

Carpenter, David and Malcolm Getz. 1994. "Evaluation of Library Resources in the Field of Economics: A Case Study." *Collection Management* 19:3, forthcoming.

Fedunok, Suzanne and Sharon Bonk. 1994. "Cooperative Acquisition and New Technologies for Resource Management and Resource Sharing: An American Model" in Ahmed H. Helal and Joachim W. Weiss, ed., *Resource Sharing: New Technologies as a Must for Universal Availability of Information* (Publications of Essen University Library 17) pp. 35-50.

Felsenthal, Edward. 1994. "New Places to Look for Legal Precedent." *Wall Street Journal*. June 1, p. B1,B5.

Getz, Malcolm. 1993. "Information Storage" in Allen Kent, ed. *Encyclopedia of Library and Information Science* LII #15, pp. 201-39.

Getz, Malcolm. forthcoming. "Petabytes of Information" *Advances in Library Administration and Organization*.

Gourman, Jack. 1993. *The Gourman Report: A Rating of Undergraduate Programs in American & International Universities*. Los Angeles: National Education Standards.

Haldeman, H. R. (Harry R.). 1994, *The Haldeman diaries*. (New York: G. P. Putnam's). CD-ROM version from SONY, 1994.

Research Library Group/Association of Research Libraries. 1993. *Interlibrary Loan Cost Study*. (Washington, D.C.: Association of Research Libraries.)

Watson, Donald Stevenson and Malcolm Getz. 1981. *Price Theory and Its Uses*. 5th edition. (Boston: Houghton Mifflin, Inc.)

The Future Using an Integrated Approach: The OhioLINK Experience

Phyllis O'Connor
Susan Wehmeyer
Susan Weldon

INTRODUCTION

Resource sharing through interlibrary loan has allowed libraries to offer access to information far beyond the walls of any one institution. Since the first interlibrary loan transaction, however, librarians have worked to reduce borrowing and lending costs and to improve delivery speed. The Ohio Library and Information Network (OhioLINK), in contract with Innovative Interfaces, Inc., is pushing the idea of resource sharing a step further.

OhioLINK's membership includes fifteen public universities, two private universities, 23 community and technical colleges and the State Library of Ohio. Its goal is to position its member libraries for the future so that it is established as the information gateway of choice for users of OhioLINK libraries. To accomplish this, the

---

Phyllis O'Connor is Assistant Dean of University Libraries at the University of Akron in Akron, OH.

Susan Wehmeyer is Head of Information Delivery Services at Fordham Health Sciences Library, Wright State University in Dayton, OH.

Susan Weldon is Head of Information Delivery Services at Paul Laurence Dunbar Library, Wright State University in Dayton, OH.

[Haworth co-indexing entry note]: "The Future Using an Integrated Approach: The OhioLINK Experience." O'Connor, Phyllis, Susan Wehmeyer, and Susan Weldon. Co-published simultaneously in *Journal of Library Administration* (The Haworth Press, Inc.) Vol. 21, No. 1/2, 1995, pp. 109-120; and *The Future of Resource Sharing* (ed: Shirley K. Baker, and Mary E. Jackson) The Haworth Press, Inc., 1995, pp. 109-120. Multiple copies of this article/chapter may be purchased from The Haworth Document Delivery Center [1-800-342-9678; 9:00 a.m. - 5:00 p.m. (EST)].

© 1995 by The Haworth Press, Inc. All rights reserved.

THE FUTURE OF RESOURCE SHARING

network will cooperatively develop collections, offer a growing number of electronic resources to all member libraries, and improve the interlibrary loan of printed material across all institutions to the point that access is virtually equivalent to ownership. Tom Sanville, Director of OhioLINK, describes the project as a work in progress which may never be finished. He believes that as technology changes and improves, so will the design of the project.

The work on this project began in 1987, when the Ohio Board of Regents began investigating the possibility of creating a state-wide automated network so that resources could easily and efficiently be shared at the state level between academic libraries.

The network that the Board of Regents envisioned would use current future technology as a tool to improve library service. Successful implementation of this program would increase the research effectiveness and productivity of faculty and students throughout the state of Ohio.

In the Fall of 1989 the Request for Proposal for OhioLINK was issued, and eight vendors responded. Innovative Interfaces, Inc. (III) was chosen in the Summer of 1990 as the vendor that could most effectively create the OhioLINK system. The committees that worked on the original proposal began working with III on the exact system configurations required to make the project work.

One of the first steps of this project was the installation of the Innovative Interfaces, Inc. integrated library system at each of the member institutions. Each local database was merged into a central catalog which was then made available for patron-initiated borrowing. The service, called online borrowing, offers patrons the opportunity to select materials from the catalogs of a growing number of institutions. The building of the central catalog started with three libraries in August 1992, and new libraries have been added at the rate of approximately one per month. The patron online borrowing function was activated in January 1994.

OhioLINK online borrowing creates a natural link between the request process and the circulation function because the patron requires no intermediary to borrow from another library. The patron online borrowing service operates as follows:

From either a terminal in the library or a remote work station, the patron identifies an item in the shared catalog which is not available locally. Users can search the central catalog in two ways: by logging directly into the central catalog or by searching their local catalog and passing their search through to the central catalog.

The patron then places a request on the public catalog to borrow that item. (The current system design only accepts requests for books with item records.) The request is electronically delivered, through the central database, to the owning library.

A paging slip, which instructs staff to pull and ship the material to the patron's library, is generated at the owning library.

The material is checked out, prepared for delivery and shipped to the borrowing library. The borrowing library receives the material and sends an arrival notice to the patron.

The transaction is recorded and updated at each step of the process on the patron's record, the owning library's item record and in the OhioLINK central catalog. The goal is to complete the service, from request to delivery, in 48-72 hours.

This article reviews how the planners and initial participants combine a patron-driven system with traditional interlibrary loan operations. It addresses the concerns and perspectives of administrators, managers and patrons, all of whom play important roles in the ongoing development of this network. Planners face issues relating to participation costs, the sharing of materials, workload and workflow management, training, and the future of interlibrary loan as a distinct operational unit.

ADMINISTRATIVE PERSPECTIVE

The concept of enhancing resource sharing through online borrowing provides administrators with a unique opportunity to expand library service, but it also presents them with major implica-

112 THE FUTURE OF RESOURCE SHARING

tions for their institutions' budgets. Some administrators are concerned about the effects of such a system on the independence of their library operations and the long-range effects of sharing their collections.

Ownership and Independence

OhioLINK planners envision a service that needs more than just cooperation and support from a diverse group of administrators. For the purposes of online borrowing, OhioLINK institutions need to function as one library with many branches. Administrators recognized the need to share more than just their online catalogs and agreed to share the bulk of their collections; however, in the early planning stages much emphasis was placed on individual ownership of books and collections. Fortunately, over the course of several years, the emphasis shifted from "my" books and "your" patrons to "our" collection and "our" patrons. Some planners even wondered whether the libraries had any reason to return material to the "owning" agency at all. Despite these thoughts, OhioLINK has not become one giant state library, even though all OhioLINK patrons do have access to all circulating collections. The acknowledged goal has been to think in terms of access rather than ownership.

Cost Issues

OhioLINK members made a commitment to develop services (e.g., patron online borrowing; access to electronic databases) which improved the cost efficiency and user effectiveness of statewide information services. The Ohio Board of Regents funds a portion of the costs for a central computer and Innovative Interfaces software at each institution; however, continued and additional funding is needed at each campus and through the OhioLINK central budget to meet the long-range goals of the project. Several funding models that rely on resources from OhioLINK, local institutions, and grants in various combinations are planned. The major financial advantage of OhioLINK, however, will be the opportunity to bring about efficiencies in the use of existing funds by economies of scale, improved processing efficiencies and reallocation of existing budgets. The major ongoing expense to local sites for improved delivery of materials will be the cost of staff time to pull, process, and ship materials. Improving efficiency will require more staff than most libraries have dedicated to the task.

OhioLINK has already offset some of the expense of improved service by centralizing common costs such as courier service, user guides, and publicity materials. The delivery service is an excellent example of how the network achieved economies of scale not attainable by individual institutions. OhioLINK locations were joined by a ground carrier system through regional hubs that offered twenty-four hour delivery between sites at a unit cost far less expensive than direct shipment methods previously used by member libraries. An initial sample placed the cost at about one dollar for each delivery to a destination.

Several additional cooperative ventures are anticipated to economize the member institutions' budgets further. When the patron borrowing function is made available for journal requests, a subsystem will centrally track usage and automatically determine copyright compliance fees. The staff time previously devoted to this task can then be reallocated. OhioLINK is also considering funding the purchase of "self check-out" stations at library locations where circulation desk staff time can be freed for other tasks. As the project progresses, improved access to other libraries' collections and an efficient collection development plan may allow administrators to make reallocations from the materials budget.

One cost issue which has not been decided is whether net lenders will be compensated for their participation. Traditional financial agreements involving interlibrary loan have emphasized balanced reciprocal borrowing. Institutions that could not supply as much as they borrowed generally paid a fee for the loan. During the first year of patron online borrowing, OhioLINK plans to analyze lending statistics and consider a formula for distributing funding based on use.

Participants resolved some cost issues related to resource sharing in administrative planning sessions. After long deliberations characterized by cooperation and consensus building, OhioLINK circulation policies were formally adopted by all members. All administrators agreed to a standard fine of fifty cents per day for overdue materials borrowed online. They also agreed to maximum fines for OhioLINK patrons who chose to borrow in person from a member library. In both cases, the lending library agreed to collect and retain these fines. The participants agreed that the borrowing library would pay the lender a standard replacement fee and processing charge for lost material. Still under discussion, however, is a plan to reduce invoicing between institutions by accounting for replacement fees on a quarterly or annual basis. To improve the recovery of long overdue items, the libraries have cooperated with student registration blocks or other available sanctions as needed.

THE OPERATING PERSPECTIVE

Local managers brought different concerns to the planning and implementation of online borrowing. They were primarily interested in workload, workflow, and training issues. They were also concerned about the impact of online borrowing on the future of interlibrary loan.

Workload and Workflow

Management staff were deeply involved in the planning process. The OhioLINK Inter-Campus Services Committee, which consisted largely of middle management staff from interlibrary loan and circulation units, was assigned the task of designing and implementing a statewide circulation system that would deliver requested materials to patrons in 48 to 72 hours. As a result, these managers learned early that successful online borrowing systems in other states had produced increased interlibrary traffic. Although managers were prepared for the need to revise workflow patterns, they had to maintain a flexible approach to the problem, because the planning process was not sufficiently detailed to allow pre-planned workflow schemes. Predictions still remain uncertain for when and at what level the workload will stabilize.

Approaches to the increased workload have varied, with member libraries employing different methods to shift the verification and ordering from library staff to patrons. The University of Akron screens all incoming interlibrary loan book requests and, when possible, uses OhioLINK online borrowing to complete transactions rather than place requests via OCLC. Akron returns the interlibrary loan form to the patron with a note encouraging the use of the OhioLINK system. Bowling Green State University returns interlibrary loan book requests to the patron when the material is available through OhioLINK with instructions to directly request the material. Wright State University advertises the new service when a patron receives an item through interlibrary loan that is available through OhioLINK. While many institutions have refrained from publicizing traditional interlibrary loan services, this new service is heavily publicized throughout the state. Library staff frequently direct patrons to the new service, but the system generally sells itself.

A related issue is the inability of the system to distribute lending requests evenly among the institutions; this is because the borrower currently selects the lending library. As a result, the participants cannot structure a reciprocal balance. Administrators at the University of Akron are understandably concerned that as the first institution listed in the holdings display, they will receive a disproportionate number of OhioLINK requests, just as they already do with OCLC lending. A system-generated algorithm to balance lending was implemented in the Fall of 1994.

Although patrons have assumed a portion of the work required to process an interlibrary loan, and patron online borrowing is less staff intensive, distribution of staff workload remains inevitably uneven. In the early stages of implementation, enthusiastic, capable staff frequently volunteered to carry a disproportionate amount of the load. As the project evolves, experienced staff will be able to take advantage of new opportunities for advancement or development which will result from restructured interlibrary loan operations. They will also play a key role in helping others adjust to changes in operation.

Training

Much of the initial staff training was through hands-on experience. On several occasions, formal training sessions were conducted by Innovative Interfaces, Inc. Participants often uncovered programming problems and changes were made by III before the training session was completed. A training database is planned, but all initial testing and training used real item records. Before testing the system, representatives agreed on standard operating procedures including: loan periods, fines, patron blocks, replacement costs, patron types and item types.

Staff at Miami University, Wright State University and University of Cincinnati gamely tested the online borrowing system before offering it to the public. Managers at these sites found items to request, created test patron accounts, tracked requested items and made printouts of everything that went right or wrong. Testing lasted nine months with no real books changing hands during the first six months. After these initial participants were trained, a partner system was implemented for testing and training. As new sites were added, each new library was paired with an experienced library. This system has been very effective.

After training key librarians at each site, only local staff training issues remained. Each OhioLINK library developed unique training methods. For example, the thirteen libraries affiliated with Wright State University used a separate but similar system III developed for intra-institutional requests. Circulation and automation services staff created screen prints and handouts that documented every step of the process. Staff placed test requests in September 1993. In November 1993, the library offered the local request function to patrons. It was an immediate success and gave staff and patrons experience with online borrowing before OhioLINK patron online borrowing was implemented.

Future of the Interlibrary Loan Unit

Throughout the planning and implementation of this new resource sharing model, the interlibrary loan librarians were concerned about what the final role of their units would be in the new system. They continue to recognize that the need for their familiar services is diminishing. Online borrowing relies upon the patron to verify the item to borrow, select the lending institution, and place the request. The computer will soon pick the item and track copyright and use statistics. Much of the rest of the borrowing and lending process can be easily folded into circulation operations or shipping/receiving units.

When the process is fully operational at all OhioLINK institutions, the management of requests through interlibrary loan may change based on the number of items requested using either online borrowing or OCLC. During the first quarter of 1994, with online borrowing available, OCLC interlibrary loan requests between OhioLINK libraries increased three percent. It is obvious that Ohio-LINK has not, so far, alleviated any of the demand for traditional interlibrary loan services. Interlibrary loan traffic patterns, however, seem to be changing. An examination of book requests being sent by the University of Akron's interlibrary loan staff shows a dramatic shift since the implementation of patron-initiated borrowing. In January 1994, the University of Akron borrowed 162 books from other OhioLINK libraries using OCLC. In March 1994, that figure was reduced to 56. By May 1994, only 29 book requests were sent. During this same five-month period, the University of Akron's patrons requested 3,570 books over the OhioLINK network.

While book borrowing decreased, journal requests and total lending temporarily increased for several reasons. First, although patrons could see journal holdings, they could not place direct requests; they needed to use interlibrary loan to request articles. Second, a number of institutions have access to the OhioLINK online catalog but are not yet able to use the patron online borrowing service. Their requests must also be processed through interlibrary loan. When journal requests are available online, and as access to the request system grows, lending via intra-OhioLINK interlibrary loan is also expected to decline. Even so, OhioLINK does not expect to satisfy all patron needs through online borrowing. The need to integrate the two processes into the organization of the library remains.

As the processes evolve, each OhioLINK library continues to struggle with the integration of online borrowing into existing organizational models. Organizational units dedicated to interlibrary loan operations have been placed in many branches of the library hierarchy. In the past, reporting structure often depended more on who was qualified to manage ILL activities in a particular library rather than on where interlibrary loan logically fit within the organizational structure. In response to the demands of online borrow-

118 THE FUTURE OF RESOURCE SHARING

ing, some OhioLINK libraries have already combined their circulation and interlibrary loan departments into one new department that deals with both functions. Others have maintained separate departments, but moved them under the same management structure, so that interlibrary loan and circulation are part of the same division.

In time, the nature of patron online borrowing may spur the development of team management in some member institutions. OhioLINK managers provide a role model for this approach by solving the inevitable glitches in a team effort. Library representatives to OhioLINK central administration continue to meet regularly to discuss issues, design testing procedures, and address other special needs. Several e-mail listserv groups have extended the avenues of communication. For example, a listserv connects the OhioLINK testers to Innovative Interfaces staff and programmers who scan problem reports and offer solutions.

Managers may also use a team approach to deal with the day-to-day practical operations of this new service while staff adjust to changes in workflow patterns, job descriptions and the stress that accompanies change. As clear departmental lines fade, it is necessary for all public service staff to have working knowledge of the online borrowing service. When a patron asks at the reference desk how to place a request on the public catalog, who will provide the instruction, simple though it is? When a patron comes to the circulation desk with the same question, will the instruction be the same? If updates to patron records were always a duty of the circulation department, but the interlibrary loan staff need updated records to fill requests, whose job will it be? The most successful online borrowing operations will involve staff with expertise in automation, traditional interlibrary loan, circulation, reference, shipping, and problem solving. If these staff do not work in the same unit or team, they must, at minimum, have a sense of working toward a common goal.

PATRON PERSPECTIVE

Generally, patrons have welcomed this new service. It is easy to use. Searches performed at the local catalog are passed through to the central catalog with a touch of a single key. Patrons request items by simply entering their name and university identification number. There are no forms to fill out, no service lines to wait in. The service is so easy to use that very little, if any, formal user education is needed; OhioLINK-issued brochures and bookmarks are sufficient teaching aids. Patrons like to use OhioLINK patron online borrowing since delivery is faster than most traditional interlibrary loan service.

Some universities have traditionally charged a fee for interlibrary loan services, and many have restricted this service to graduate students and faculty members. However, OhioLINK online borrowing of books is offered without charge to every undergraduate and graduate student, faculty and affiliated faculty, staff, and courtesy card holder at every OhioLINK institution. Predictions that graduate and faculty use of the online borrowing function would far exceed undergraduate use have proven untrue. Figures for the first five months of OhioLINK borrowing show that of the over 24,000 requests placed across the system that graduate students borrowed 9,529 books (38.2% of the total traffic); that undergraduates borrowed 7,915 (31.7%); and that faculty borrowed 5,301 (21.2%). The remainder of the requests (8.4%) were placed mostly by staff.

Although it is too early for real statistical analysis of changing patron behavior, anecdotal evidence of such change exists. A graduate assistant at an OhioLINK site cheerfully selected books from another OhioLINK library to avoid searching the stacks. This same graduate assistant located journal titles at OhioLINK libraries and placed her requests through Interlibrary Loan to avoid the cost involved in photocopying at her institution. "This way," she reported, "I can come back in a few days, and pick up my photocopies and books all in one place, and I'll be all set." Some patrons were observed "hedging their bets" to secure a particularly popular book. They requested ALL available copies "just to be sure." Because the online catalog encourages "electronic browsing," many patrons request books just to examine the index or table of contents. Unlike the familiar and unchanging card catalog of yesteryear, versions of computer software enter and leave the library as though through a revolving door. As a result, patrons of the 1990s learn to adapt very quickly to change. As the above examples illustrate, OhioLINK patrons have been quick to accept and exploit the changes and opportunities created by patron online borrowing.

CONCLUSION

Futurists envision researchers in the twenty-first century, browsing topical "libraries" at will, while a computer in direct interface with the human brain identifies relevant reading material. A likely article is instantly downloaded to a small electronic "book." When a question arises in the lab, a quick link to the International Library provides the answer. Although such wonders exist only in science fiction books today, expanding consumer demand for information may drive technology to make fiction reality before we know it.

Despite the lure and glamour of the future, we still live in a time when books and journals are published in print; when libraries must buy individual copies and subscriptions; and when librarians must cope with copyright guidelines, reciprocal agreements, and lending policies. Obtaining resources from outside the walls of the library, whether under the banner of interlibrary loan, document delivery or resource sharing, is the reality of today.

Through OhioLINK, member institutions are addressing their present needs while developing their roles in the future information industry; they are becoming a connective gateway offering valuable access and convenient packaging at library network costs; they plan to provide full-text databases linked to citation databases; they also plan to find alternative technologies for document delivery (e.g., patron online borrowing of journal articles and UMI "Power Pages" article delivery). Integrating online borrowing with interlibrary loan is just the first step in an ongoing process. It is a step towards bridging the gap from today to the future.

Impact of Holdings on Resource Sharing

Julie Wessling

This paper will explore the issues surrounding the impacts of holdings on resource sharing, and identify options for providing users with efficient access to materials. A case can be made for using the term "access" to describe any department or service in a library—access to materials, access to bibliographic records, access to location assistance, access to local collections, access to other collections, access to the information highway, and so on. Then again, the information highway provides access to information, electronic publishers provide access to information, information brokers provide access to information, and commercial document suppliers provide access to information. So, what is the difference? What do libraries have that other information access points lack? That is easy: collections. Well, not exactly easy; in fact, collections are becoming increasingly troublesome, beginning with the basic task of defining them. Let's stop right there—defining them. That is where holdings and access come together. In order for users to experience a seamless circle of access to information, the definition of collections suddenly incorporates a description of both holdings and access.

Resource sharing magnifies the integrated nature of holdings and access. On site, a user can make some use of a collection regardless of access to holdings information. However, it is impossible to

---

Julie Wessling is Assistant Director for Public Services at Colorado State University Libraries in Fort Collins, CO.

[Haworth co-indexing entry note]: "Impact of Holdings on Resource Sharing." Wessling, Julie. Co-published simultaneously in *Journal of Library Administration* (The Haworth Press, Inc.) Vol. 21, No. 1/2, 1995, pp. 121-131; and *The Future of Resource Sharing* (ed: Shirley K. Baker, and Mary E. Jackson) The Haworth Press, Inc., 1995, pp. 121-131. Multiple copies of this article/chapter may be purchased from The Haworth Document Delivery Center [1-800-342-9678; 9:00 a.m. - 5:00 p.m. (EST)].

© 1995 by The Haworth Press, Inc. All rights reserved.

request material efficiently from remote collections without access to holdings information about items available. Conversely, it is likely that requests for loan of material will increase when holdings information on a collection is accessible from a variety of places. And the number of requests will be a result of both the number and nature of holdings in a specific collection.

COLLECTION BUILDING

To quote Peter Senge, "The 20th century will be seen as a revolution–from seeing the world as one primarily made of things to one that is fundamentally made up of relationships."[1]

In order to take advantage of relationships among libraries, it is essential to reorient collection development. Cooperative collection building must become more than just a myth; libraries need to embrace a plan to collectively meet the needs of their users. Librarians should move past thinking in terms of "my patrons" and begin to develop a shared vision around meeting the needs of "our patrons." How much planning is currently occurring to fill the gaps that already exist and will surely get worse as a result of massive serial cuts and significant reduction or even elimination of monographic purchases? How will libraries meet the demand years down the road for the increasing number of rarely held items?

Cancellations and decreased purchasing power are causing library collections to look more and more alike, as libraries are reduced to buying essential materials that support only the most basic user needs. Academic institutions are building duplicate libraries which support instruction in the core programs; public libraries are adding titles in specific collections which are becoming increasingly predictable across a similar population base. Alarmingly, our similar collections are also building common gaps which will surely increase and become more difficult to fill as time passes.

There is need right now to address this issue locally, statewide, regionally, and nationally. Collection building needs to incorporate consortial, regional and national efforts to build comprehensive holdings collectively with a commitment to provide access. There are some libraries that promise rapid fax or electronic delivery of journal literature.[2] In other cases, libraries agree to share remote storage for infrequently circulated holdings.[3] Libraries need to make a binding commitment to maintain these lesser held items, to provide bibliographic access on regional and national databases, and to provide provision for the actual delivery of requested material.

It is important that national bibliographic utilities, and local system interconnectivity, be encouraged and maintained in order to support access to holdings information. Self-contained stand-alone databases mean no one else outside the system knows what is available. There is need to lobby for government assistance, such as Library Services and Construction Act (LSCA) funds, to encourage and support participation in national utilities and/or facilitate seamless connections among regional or local systems.

Nonexistent or incomplete access to serial holdings information remains a serious impediment to efficient resource sharing. Issue-specific holdings information greatly facilitates efficient access, as demonstrated by high interlibrary loan (ILL) fill rates when these data are available. Perhaps the best example of cooperative control of serials is DOCLINE, the NLM-automated ILL system for medical libraries, where 80% of the contributing libraries report specific serial holdings. Because of this high level of participation, DOCLINE boasts an impressive ILL fill rate of 92% to 99%; the majority of requests are satisfied on the first or second location. DOCLINE links directly with SERHOLD, which indicates the specific holdings of each library owning a bibliographic title. This permits ILL requests to be routed automatically to libraries coded for the needed issue. The importance of standardized serials holdings information is demonstrated by the markedly lower fill rates among the medical libraries with nonstandardized holdings information (not ANSI standard 1980, level 3). When a library has nonstandardized data, DOCLINE assigns a request based on whether a journal is currently published and whether the library has a current subscription. Even when these two requirements are met, up to 8% of the routed requests are unfilled because of incomplete holdings.[4,5] It is important that holdings information be included in all state, regional, and national bibliographic efforts. The efficiency rate drops dramatically for any cooperative sharing of journal titles without issue-specific information. In addition, it becomes impossi-

124 THE FUTURE OF RESOURCE SHARING

ble to guarantee that all volumes of a journal are available long term when libraries are forced to enter into serial cancellation efforts. A new challenge is to have holdings information incorporate alternative delivery options.

As libraries achieve success in integrating holdings and information on delivery options, they gain an invaluable bartering tool for maintaining leadership and control in the delivery of information. Uniform, networked holdings information, including data for serials, monographs and other formats, will allow libraries to enter into cooperative agreements to meet the needs of their combined clientele.

ACCESS TO NETWORKED HOLDINGS

Resource sharing assumes that library users will routinely have the means to identify and locate needed material. Increasingly, this ability is developing unevenly among libraries, and existing efforts are being overshadowed by commercial-based electronic options with high user appeal. Librarians should move quickly to create procedures that embrace these various electronic alternatives and have libraries concentrate local initiatives on integrating unique holdings into the access loop. This will include the design of gateways and interfaces that facilitate document retrieval from library collections as well as from commercial document suppliers, full-text databases, and electronic publishers. All databases should include the connection between an identified bibliographic citation and the specified document, with links to alternative delivery options.

As options proliferate, it becomes more important for users to have a single source for assistance in identifying choices. This need provides the opportunity for libraries to combine their role to provide bibliographic control for information with their role to provide training and support services for users. These two primary goals provide the base to formulate a library-wide vision for all staff to cooperate in providing efficient access to materials. This shared vision needs to focus on providing the user with facilitated access to information, regardless of its location, and build the framework for libraries to be primary nodes in any information network.

There are examples reported in the literature of libraries expanding access to select holdings in a variety of ways. Libraries are automating their check-in and holdings records and adding local holdings data to CD-ROM and online databases to identify locally held materials. The libraries of the University of Tennessee, Knoxville (UTK) have developed an innovative method to manage the expanding number of alternatives for accessing specific titles by development of the Electronic Journal List (EJL). EJL is a database developed using dBASEIII+; it identifies journals available electronically, including information about the host system, file name, time coverage of the online journal, and holdings for UTK library subscription. This provides users with online information about alternative access to a select number of journal titles.[6]

The integration of interfaces and gateways in the library OPAC creates more sophisticated access. Carnegie Mellon University provides an electronic library prototype with its Mercury project. The OPAC and a variety of databases, including locally produced databases and vendor databases, are available remotely. There is a single search interface for all these. MELVYL (the University of California nine-campus online union catalog) and OhioLINK (linking 18 academic libraries in Ohio) extend these interfaces into a shared consortial environment. Users of MELVYL and OhioLINK not only have access to a variety of online databases and delivery options, but also may initiate requests for delivery of materials held in the collections of participating libraries.

Add OCLC's FirstSearch or RLG's Eureka to the mix of options, and in no time the typical user has access to a rapidly growing number of full-text databases as well as online abstracts and indexing tools linked directly to commercial delivery options. Or, add a gateway to CARL Corporation's UnCover, which provides table of contents access to a mushrooming number of titles coupled with fax delivery of articles found, and, more recently, any articles regardless of year for journal titles in the database. The gateway, for a fee, can be customized to reflect local holdings information.

Simultaneously, some libraries are concentrating on developing sophisticated "virtual libraries" in specialized subject areas. A premier example of this is Project Janus at the Columbia University Law Library.[7] The project includes electronic scanning, digitizing,

126 THE FUTURE OF RESOURCE SHARING

and indexing of every item in the collection, nearly three-quarters of a million volumes of legal material. Ultimately the system will allow the user to browse through exact images of items in the collection and also search for specific pieces of information in any of the documents.

And, off to the side, but quickly gathering speed and momentum as they move to center stage, are projects exploring electronic journal publishing. These include The University LIcensing Program (TULIP) with Elsevier Science Publishers, which provides network access to digital images of selected science journals, and the Red Sage project which includes two dozen publishers working with AT&T Bell Laboratories to develop a commercial electronic document distribution system called the RightPages. These projects provide full image electronic access to articles directly from the publisher. Currently, these projects deal with a small segment of journal publishing; many believe electronic delivery of journal articles will soon become a mainstream service, available for most titles. As copyright issues are clarified and workstation requirements become more affordable, many users will expect nothing less than direct delivery of article images to a local personal computer.

It will be up to librarians to package access to library holdings seamlessly into this array of information sources. Although librarians need to play a leadership role both in creating bibliographic access and in providing training and support services for users of network information, it is essential that they approach these tasks in partnership with all information providers. Librarians can lead by championing standards for interconnectivity along with equality of access for all users, but also by carefully defining the most effective focus for their own finite resources.

Commercial suppliers are in business for profit, and what they make available for document delivery will be driven by market demand for specific titles. Librarians can take advantage of these alternative access options evolving for users to obtain high demand material, and redirect library resources to address the long term needs of scholars and researchers for specialized, esoteric, rare, or foreign publications.

The successful management of user access to information requires integration of planned access to materials available in electronic format with planned reliance on jointly built collections in libraries for print materials and specialized collections. For library holdings, it is especially important not to lose sight of information that will likely never be available electronically. Such items include very specialized or esoteric publications aimed at small audiences and large numbers of retrospective materials currently held in libraries and not demonstrating high-level demand. This is where successful cooperative collection development and cooperative collection weeding are most critical. These items are at high risk of becoming "lost" from both the access and delivery paths.

ROLE OF ILL

ILL provides a model of the successful transfer of resources among libraries to serve individual user needs. We have an opportunity to expand this traditional role to include planned delivery of identified resources held not only in libraries, but also stored in electronic databases or distributed through commercial services. The process of merging traditional ILL service with a full range of document delivery options allows provision of the single-point access service that the user desires.

Only libraries possess retrospective holdings, a critical element in the information access equation. Gateways and interfaces are needed to facilitate document retrieval from library collections as well as from commercial document sources. Where the requested material is obtained, whether from the local library, another library, an electronic information bank, or a commercial supplier, is not of concern to the patron as long as requirements of document quality, time, and cost are met.[8]

In a sophisticated user-centered document delivery system, the user has a perception of accessing a single source or library. A user is able to order material, regardless of its location, and have it delivered directly to his or her home or office. Ideally, this system should support routing mechanisms sensitive to local parameters and also equalize load distribution of requests. It should route requests based on item-specific holdings information. This could be designed in a manner similar to the routing mechanism described above for DOCLINE, which enhances retrieval and delivery options based on specific holdings information which is automatically matched with each request for high level efficiency. The system should also electronically match requests with consortial or other agreement priorities and check for circulation status. And, the process should accommodate linking local call number information as each request is imported into a local library system for handling.

This routing mechanism should incorporate not only libraries, but also commercial delivery options or full-text or electronic delivery alternatives. An important use of the *ARL/RLG ILL Cost Study*, which identifies the borrowing and lending costs for 76 U.S. and Canadian research libraries, is to indicate economical alternatives. The data are most frequently cited to determine when it is best to buy, catalog and maintain an item, and when it is more cost-effective to borrow it or go to a commercial supplier. The cost study data will help identify lending as well as borrowing options. For example, at Colorado State we are considering screening of lending requests to route all article requests as appropriate to UnCover for handling. This would be a less expensive option in many cases, even if we subsidized the fee as appropriate for consortial partners. Fulfillment of significant numbers of requests by electronic means or by commercial suppliers will help libraries address the current unevenness in levels of lending and borrowing among libraries. This change in policy will allow collective efficiency in use of library resources. Then, staff resources can be allocated to fill only requests which lack non-library suppliers; fees will be based on the relationship and agreements of the specific libraries.

Successful negotiation of consortial agreements will require the blurring of lines between traditional ILL and collection development activities. As mentioned above, libraries should seek binding commitments to maintain lesser held items and to provide bibliographic access. These agreements need to reflect specific delivery options and be developed to facilitate user-initiated ordering. Commercial alternatives may frequently be the most cost-effective choice; however, in order to recognize the full financial advantage, the system design should be such that the user "pushes the button," and library staff time is eliminated at both ends of the process.

Again, any patron request system should link with a variety of alternatives; the user should only be required to indicate that something is needed. Automatic routing and computerized decision trees would facilitate filling a specific request in the most efficient way possible. This could be expanded to include a rapid order option when the item is something which should appropriately be added to the local collection. Perhaps this could involve a direct link with a local bookstore or vendor for onshelf material which can be delivered immediately. In order to integrate this option successfully into a user-centered electronic request system, there would have to be a point of decision which could electronically link with a management system and review criteria, including:

- How often has this item been ordered?
- Does it match approval/purchase plan profile?
- Are there dollars remaining in this subject area allocation?
- Does it fall within librarian-defined price parameters?
- Is it already held or on order from another source?
- Is it held by consortial or other special partners?

The rapid ordering module should be designed to "kick out" requests that lack any of the necessary requirements. These items could be reviewed for purchase; however, the actual request would continue on to another supplier for fulfillment in order to expedite receipt for the individual requestor.

As routine requests are handled by commercial suppliers and/or automated patron-generated modules, a smaller core of requests will demand in-depth searching or handling by ILL staff. Will it then become possible to "share" ILL expertise, perhaps having one ILL guru per consortium of libraries? Or will these requests lend themselves to outsourcing? For example, a central bibliographic utility might handle verification, identification of locations, negotiation of loan requirements, and fees, ideally coupled with sending the item directly from the supplying library to the end user.

Technology will increase options rapidly. As users experience these options, libraries need to complement them, not compete with them. It will be up to libraries to maintain necessary links and act as mediators where required. Lack of holdings will continue to be a problem. However, the traditional reasons for lacking needed material, including small collections, specialized collections, temporary non-availability status, and non-circulating status, will all be minimized as we move into an electronic networked environment which will continue to augment access with alternative delivery options. These new possibilities promise to allow ILL staff to focus energy on only those requests which demand library interaction. Resource sharing will flourish as turnaround times shrink. We must encourage national protocols and standards which support planned dependence on commercial and electronic document suppliers. Inter-dependency among libraries, commercial suppliers, and publishers will allow us to be mutually successful.

CONCLUSION

Partnerships including groups of libraries, commercial document suppliers, and publishers will be most successful. We can no longer afford to act independently. Holdings will become increasingly important as a bartering tool to gain additional access benefits; stand-alone, non-circulating collections will become dinosaurs. The emerging new environment will require examination of all aspects of operation, including policies, procedures, staffing patterns, use of resources and, most importantly, external relationships. Expectations for the near future include the following:

1. Bartering potential will become a basic criterion for local collection building.
2. Cooperative collection building among consortial partners will redefine lending options, with all items becoming eligible for loan or scanned for electronic delivery.
3. Library collections will be valued for their uniqueness and for their defined, binding relationships to other libraries and to electronic alternatives.
4. There will be financial incentives for consortial, state, or regional agreements to collect, maintain, and deliver materials which have been purchased to meet a common vision.
5. Bibliographic control will incorporate option(s) for delivery of items.
6. Holdings information will be solidly linked with delivery option(s). Holdings without a delivery option will be defined separately from the rest of the collection.

7. ILL verification will cease to be a two step process of verifying the item first and the location second; except in rare cases, this information will be packaged together.
8. User-centered request systems will predominate.
9. Libraries will universally charge for lending materials; "charges" will incorporate consortial or bartering agreements and vary with relationships.
10. Libraries will cease to honor ILL requests for items available from vendors.

AUTHOR NOTE

Julie Wessling has written a number of articles and has given presentations on automated ILL and document delivery issues. Before being named Assistant Director, she was the ILL librarian at CSU and under her leadership the department developed an ILL electronic request system, which has been enhanced to link with the OCLC ILL subsystem package.

NOTES

1. Senge, Peter. *Globe & Mail*, May 4, 1993.
2. Perryman, W. R. "The changing landscape of information access: The impact of technological advances upon the acquisition, ownership, and dissemination of informational resources within the research library community," the *Journal of Library Administration* 15 (1991): 73-93.
3. Huston, Mary M. and Robert Skinner. "Information networking issues and initiatives: the North Texas experience." In *Resource Sharing: New Technologies as a must for Universal Availability of Information,* 16th International Essen Symposium, 18 October-21 October 1993 (Essen: Universitates biblioteck Essen, 1994). pp. 51-60.
4. Colaianni, L. A. "DOCLINE: The National Library of Medicine experience." In *Riding the Electronic Wave-Document Delivery: Proceedings of the Library of Congress Network Advisory Committee Meeting, November 29-December 1, 1989* (Network Planning Paper, no. 20) Washington D.C., Library of Congress 1990. pp. 33-36.
5. Hill, S., "Growth of Communication Systems among biomedical libraries." In *Research Access through Technology* edited by Mary E. Jackson. New York, AMS Press, 1989. pp. 47-55.
6. Gillikin, D.P. "Document delivery from full-text online files: A pilot project." *Online* 14 (1990): 27-32.
7. Pare, Roger. "Manuscripts and megabytes: The future of Columbia Libraries." *Columbia* (Fall 1993): 32-35.
8. Wessling, Julie. "Document delivery: A primary service for the nineties," *Advances in Librarianship* 16 (1992): 1-31.

Commercial Document Delivery: The Academic Library's Perspective

Nancy S. Hewison
Vicki J. Killion
Suzanne M. Ward

INTRODUCTION

Many factors contribute to the explosive growth in demand for document delivery services. Patrons enjoy increasingly easy access to growing numbers of electronic and CD-ROM databases and, thus, easier and faster access to larger numbers of document citations. New resources, technology, document formats, patron expectations, and library network agreements constantly suggest new service and delivery options in an environment in which everyone seems to want more documents faster than ever, while most libraries' materials budgets shrink every year. To meet patrons' needs and expectations, access services librarians in universities and colleges struggle to meet the challenge of providing fast, easy, accurate, and cost-effective document delivery from an ever widening range of sources.

Nancy S. Hewison is Planning Librarian, and Associate Professor of Library Science at the Purdue University Libraries in West Lafayette, IN.

Vicki J. Killion is Pharmacy, Nursing and Health Sciences Librarian, and Associate Professor of Library Science at the Purdue University Libraries in West Lafayette, IN.

Suzanne M. Ward is Head of Access Services, Purdue University Libraries in West Lafayette, IN.

[Haworth co-indexing entry note]: "Commercial Document Delivery: The Academic Library's Perspective." Hewison, Nancy S., Vicki J. Killion, and Suzanne M. Ward. Co-published simultaneously in *Journal of Library Administration* (The Haworth Press, Inc.) Vol. 21, No. 1/2, 1995, pp. 133-143; and *The Future of Resource Sharing* (ed: Shirley K. Baker, and Mary E. Jackson) The Haworth Press, Inc., 1995, pp. 133-143. Multiple copies of this article/chapter may be purchased from The Haworth Document Delivery Center [1-800-342-9678; 9:00 a.m. - 5:00 p.m. (EST)].

© 1995 by The Haworth Press, Inc. All rights reserved.

In its broadest definition, document delivery means providing copies of information requests in any format and from any source. "Any source" includes campus collections, commercial publishers, trade or professional associations, government agencies, fulltext databases, universities, library fee-based information services, commercial document delivery firms, information brokers, companies, and individual researchers. For this article, however, "document delivery" means the provision of print documents from for-profit, commercial suppliers that provide print or electronic holdings information. This definition includes firms such as the Institute for Scientific Information (ISI), UnCover, University Microfilms International (UMI), and Engineering Information, but excludes organizations such as the British Library Document Supply Centre (a library), the National Technical Information Service (a government agency), or the American Institute of Aeronautics and Astronautics' photocopy service (a professional association). Non-profit services also provide document delivery, which in many cases complements the commercial services' inventory, but for this article, the focus is on for-profit firms.

DOCUMENT DELIVERY SERVICE POLICIES

Few libraries provide everything to everyone, and at no cost. A library document delivery service will be no exception. Many colleagues predict, and in some cases already practice, a program in which levels of service and cost are predetermined. A library might provide basic, premium, and deluxe services, each with guidelines on eligible users, what is provided, materials supplied, use of potential suppliers, and the format and cost of provided document.

Basic service may be viewed as the current interlibrary loan service, but with minor modifications. Suppliers are consortia members who generally provide documents free of charge to members. Authorized users include the institution's faculty, staff, and students.

Premium service may offer the range of document types, but differs from basic service in that library staff select non-primary suppliers and/or may pay a premium to obtain material to meet a user's rush deadline. Online citation verification may also be included in this category. The library would charge fees for all or some premium services.

Deluxe, or value-added, service may follow the fee-based model of the Purdue University Libraries' Technical Information Service (TIS), a full-service, cost-recovery information provider. TIS locates, copies or purchases, and delivers the document according to customer preferences. Most current customers are from the business community, but in the future, academic libraries may well offer this service to anyone willing to pay the price of "instant" information gratification.

The most cost effective way to charge for these services is to establish a fee schedule designed to ensure cost recovery for the entire program rather than billing actual costs for each of thousands of individual items. The library would assess additional charges for the "extras," such as faxing or file transfer.

Policies of the deluxe service will probably resemble current interlibrary loan policies. Librarians should evaluate the existing service, retain what works well, and improve upon what does not. They should clarify the same basic questions: who will be allowed to use the service; what will be supplied; who will supply the document; when or in what time frame will it be supplied; how will it be delivered; and at what cost?

Some interlibrary loan departments have historically served faculty and graduate students, but not undergraduates. As subject-specific bibliographic databases are integrated into online catalogs, undergraduates will demand documents not held locally. Unless an academic library makes the improbable and fiscally impossible commitment to subscribe to all the publications included in these databases, librarians will assume an even more active role in helping undergraduates to select locally held documents and to request others when appropriate. If services are fee-based and time-related, however, many undergraduates will exclude themselves from using access services.

If libraries use commercial document suppliers as alternate sources for current journal subscriptions, the majority of requests will probably be copies of journal articles. But what about government reports, conference proceedings, patents? These items often require additional staff time to verify and locate. While it is theoretically possible eventually to obtain copies of most items patrons request, each library must set its own limits. What are reasonable turnaround times, costs, and document formats? How far will staff go, within flexible limits, to obtain an item? If a cost exceeds a pre-set upper limit beyond which the library will not absorb costs, should interlibrary loan offer to act as a purchasing agent, obtain the item, and pass the charge along to the patron? And what are the costs? Just the document fee? Or also some of the staff time, phone calls, and online costs needed to identify the document and its supplier? At what point in the library's investment in this process does an item cross the line from being a single-user request to becoming a potential addition to the collection? A tiered offering of services may partially solve this problem.

A library that offers a tiered menu of services may select a library supplier to fill "basic" service requests and a non-library organization for "premium" or "deluxe" requests, thus eliminating case-by-case decisions. All but the largest libraries will probably limit themselves to one or two major commercial document delivery firms and to a dozen organizations to supply specialized items (e.g., patents, technical reports, government publications, and industry standards). Decisions to pursue the remaining small percentage of requests by contacting publishers, authors, trade associations, university departments, or individual government agencies would rest with the users, based on their need for the material and their willingness to pay the fees for deluxe service.

The adage "time is money" can easily be adopted for a document delivery service. The sooner the user needs an item, the more expensive it will be to deliver. The basic price for the material usually remains constant; the value-added portion of search, retrieval, and delivery is the price differential. Perhaps just as important as speed of delivery is the process through which a user must request a document. If, for example, the library offers a table-of-contents service to provide access to current journals, then a document request mechanism should be integrated (so that the user is unaware of the ultimate source of the delivered item). The time required to place an order, both by the user and the library, should be as important as retrieval time.

SELECTING AND EVALUATING SUPPLIERS

It will be a long time before libraries completely abandon traditional interlibrary loan channels for obtaining at least some of the documents unavailable at the home institution. Commercial suppliers' inventory is currently limited by year, material format, material type, subject coverage, and language. For example, subject coverage is often weaker in the humanities, and conference proceedings, if available, are not as comprehensive as journal backfiles. In addition, documents obtained from commercial suppliers often cost more than those obtained via interlibrary loan. These factors mean, at least in the short term, that libraries should not jettison current interlibrary loan partnerships in favor of alternative document suppliers.

Many interlibrary loan departments test several commercial suppliers on a trial basis before making a final decision. The two major features to track are order processing, and record keeping or accounting. Order processing features include turnaround time; percentage of requests filled; accurate order fulfillment; quality photocopies; prompt notification of cancelled orders; ability to accept orders in a variety of ways (phone, fax, electronic mail, Dialorder, and/or OCLC or RLIN); ability to deliver documents in a variety of ways (mail, fax, and/or various overnight courier services); timely and accurate handling of rush requests; and a very low error rate combined with the willingness and ability to correct any errors quickly and accurately. Record keeping or accounting features include the ability to cite reference numbers on invoices; ability to generate customized usage reports if required; consistent pricing in accordance with published fee schedules; helpful staff; ability to track orders and provide status reports; and accurate, clear, and timely invoices.

Any test should last at least six months for library staff to gather enough information about each supplier's performance to decide which firm best meets the library's needs. In addition, a long test period gives the supplier data about the library's volume of requests; these figures may help if the library negotiates special rates based on anticipated volume. The library document delivery manager should select one or, at most, two primary commercial document providers, along with an appropriate assortment of secondary suppliers for specialized documents.

Many librarians prefer using deposit accounts to handle payments for major document suppliers since only a few checks need be prepared each year. Staff should still monitor monthly statements, first to be sure that charges are accurate, and then to compile statistics about the supplier's average document turnaround time and price. Periodic evaluations should be made to determine whether the supplier still meets the library's expectations. Staff should keep informed of new players or of new products or delivery mechanisms from established suppliers. Managers should also explore volume discount options with major suppliers. Discount rates are often part of the suppliers' published rates, but an institution or consortium which is a high volume customer might be able to negotiate even better rates.

COLLECTION DEVELOPMENT IMPLICATIONS

The ideal collection development policy integrates the institution's changing long-term priorities while meeting the current research and educational goals of the faculty and students. Continual quality improvement or intervention (CQI) is a management technique currently popular in nursing and other professions. Implementing changes through CQI provides improved quality control on an ongoing basis. Collection development in an era of diminishing funds and expanding information delivery services requires librarians to adopt a rigorous CQI stance. The addition of a table-of-contents service or document delivery service into a library's online system offers users a seemingly endless stream of information. Librarians should continually monitor user access activity to anticipate changes in research directions and to support decisions to move from document delivery to acquisitions or vice versa.

The subject specialist's responsibility for monitoring the existing collection will expand to include following trends in document delivery. Decisions to add materials based upon document usage patterns call for interaction between subject specialists and the access services manager. Reports generated either by the vendors or by internal document delivery units will provide data for ongoing collection development based upon documents ordered.

Flexibility within the acquisitions process will be needed to cancel or acquire new titles quickly. Some funds once used to maintain subscriptions will be shifted to support direct delivery of information to the user. One difficult aspect will be explaining to university administrators and accountants that a document is actually a part of that intangible "service" that costs money, but that cannot be quantified in concrete collected assets. Accrediting bodies will also have to be educated on this point. Access services provides ways for libraries to achieve cost containment, but not necessarily cost savings.

INNOVATIONS

There are several ways that a library might use the services of commercial document delivery suppliers. Jackson recently presented five ways of effectively integrating commercial document delivery with interlibrary loan services.[1] In the most traditional model, a library uses commercial suppliers only after eliminating other libraries as potential lenders. In a reverse model, the library chooses commercial suppliers first. In a third model, the library provides access to table-of-contents or citation databases which allow patrons not only to identify desired documents but also to request and receive them independently of the library. Some libraries, Jackson suggests, may make this access available only to certain groups of users, with the document needs of other groups served by the interlibrary loan department. Finally, libraries and commercial suppliers are pioneering fulltext access to documents stored electronically. Two innovative library programs explore other issues related to document delivery.

Gelman Library at the George Washington University (GW) is a library actively exploring a new balance between anticipatory collection building and on-demand delivery of information. At GW, the library has taken significant steps toward just-in-time access by creating "a service that would provide access to the journal literature that is as good as having volumes on the shelf."[2] In establishing the Scholars' Express service, librarians have divided the journal literature into three tiers. The first, "core collection," is the locally held journal collection. Those titles that fall outside the library's collection development policy form another tier, from which articles will be acquired through traditional interlibrary loan. Between these two tiers lie those journals that fit the collection policies, but are not locally held due to cancellation or non-subscription. For these titles, Scholars' Express provides a copy of any journal article, as rapidly as possible and at no charge to the user. Commercial suppliers, such as UMI and UnCover, fill most of the Scholars' Express requests. During the program's first year, the library funded Scholars' Express from an increase in the base budget granted by the university to "move toward an 'access budget'."[3] Since then, the Collections Access budget has been a portion of the overall collections budget.

The Purdue University Libraries allow faculty to place electronic orders for journal articles identified by searching ISI's Current Contents on Diskette® (CCOD) on the Libraries' server.[4] Users search or browse CCOD and save relevant references, which they forward as electronic mail to the interlibrary loan office. After screening out requests that can be filled locally, this office electronically forwards the remaining orders to The Genuine Article® (TGA) service at ISI. The Libraries currently absorb costs for TGA document delivery, as well as for copies of journal articles from its own collection. Most items obtained via other commercial suppliers and traditional interlibrary loan are also free to users.

FUTURE DIRECTIONS

The ideal document delivery system, from the viewpoint of many librarians and users, would feature a transparent, seamless electronic service incorporating searching and browsing, identification and marking of desired items, and transmission and fulfillment of requests. Items would be supplied from library collections, commercial suppliers, or other sources, without the requester knowing where the item was located. Users might then receive documents as fulltext electronic files, fax copies, or mailed print copies. Implicit in such a system would be a number of automatic features: verifying the user's eligibility; checking requests against local and consortia holdings, and/or the inventory lists of commercial suppliers; and routing the request to the appropriate supplier, which may be the home institution's access services office. The ideal system would also incorporate record keeping and accounting functions, including verification that an item had been received. Additionally, a browsability feature would allow the user to preview selected portions of the article. A version of this scenario, minus the library involvement, may already be a reality on a very small scale for users needing a limited range of documents and having their own accounts with one or two specialized document suppliers. For the vast majority of academic users, however, librarians will continue to act as intermediaries for document delivery.

In current practice, librarians prefer a wide range of options for ordering items from commercial document suppliers. They want to use whatever forms and transmission media are the most convenient for their individual operations. Even in an electronic era, librarians still need an accountability trail. For example, while it may be faster and cheaper for a commercial supplier to fax an article directly to the end user, the interlibrary loan office requires simultaneous notification that the order was filled to approve the subsequent invoice and to follow up with the supplier if the user has any questions about the order.

As collections shrink, librarians will pay even closer attention to the relationship between document delivery and collection development. At the very least, they will want to monitor overall usage by journal title. Additional value-added features might include tracking by academic department or correlations between journal subscription price and the number of article requests from each journal title. Librarians may ask commercial document suppliers to produce detailed, customized reports about their institutions' usage patterns. Consortium members using the same primary document supplier may want periodic reports comparing usage between institutions. The final decision about selecting a primary document supplier may rest on this factor, assuming that other factors, such as price and turnaround time, are relatively consistent among suppliers. To avoid the higher costs of having to track and compile usage in-house, librarians should be prepared to pay for special reports. Commercial firms should take the initiative to design and promote these services. In the short term, a document delivery firm might lose revenue by providing a report that shows that it would be more cost-ef-

142 THE FUTURE OF RESOURCE SHARING

fective for a library to subscribe to or reinstate a certain journal title. However, in the long term, this lost revenue would be more than made up by the library's continued use of the document delivery service, especially when further serial titles are cut.

Many firms offer, or are developing, bibliographic databases that can be mounted on their academic customers' mainframes and searched by authorized end users. Easy document ordering features are often built into the software. Librarians welcome this feature, but would appreciate better links between the vendors' databases and the local or consortium online catalog. They also want to avoid situations in which their institutions pay for commercial document supply of hundreds or thousands of articles from material already available on the library shelves. The ideal software would compare the user's document request with the online catalog and immediately indicate ownership and holdings. The software would block the user from ordering the item from the commercial supplier, although it would allow ordering from the library's campus document delivery service. Access services staff would be able to override the block if they later determined that the article was indeed unavailable locally. The catalog checking software should be much more sophisticated than current offerings; for example, it should reliably match bibliographic database conference records with ISBN numbers to the corresponding online catalog conference records that have been cataloged with ISSN numbers.

Each academic library is unique in its mix of funding, collections, service philosophy, objectives, staffing, student body, scholastic programs, size, and faculty research patterns. Given shrinking library budgets, most librarians will soon have to make decisions about using non-traditional document delivery sources, if they have not already done so. The constantly changing environment of new technology, new suppliers, new services, and new patron expectations will make these choices challenging. More staff will be involved in or affected by the decisions than just those in interlibrary loan or access services. Librarians and staff in collection development, serials, reference, automation, and acquisitions will daily feel the impact of these new document delivery options.

REFERENCES

1. Jackson, Mary E. "Integrating ILL with Document Delivery: Five Models." *Wilson Library Bulletin* 68, 1993: 76-8.

2. Bezanson, Deborah K., and Lee Anne George. "Scholars' Express: Just in Time Access to Journal Literature." Poster session presented at the Association of College and Research Libraries' Sixth National Conference, Salt Lake City, April 12-14, 1992.

3. Masters, Deborah. "Access and Ownership: Issues and Financing." Panel presentation at the Association of College and Research Libraries' Sixth National Conference, Salt Lake City, April 12-14, 1992.

4. Kerr, Richard Cary, Nancy S. Hewison, and Vicki J. Killion. "Multi-User Access to a DOS-Based Program Via UNIX: the Purdue University Libraries Current Contents on Diskette (R) Project." In *Proceedings of the Fifteenth National Online Meeting*, edited by Martha E. Williams. pp. 249-55. Medford, NJ: Learned Information, 1994.

System Architecture and Networking Issues in Implementing the North American Interlibrary Loan and Document Delivery (NAILDD) Initiative

Clifford A. Lynch

INTRODUCTION

The Association of Research Libraries has undertaken a major initiative called the North American Interlibrary Loan and Document Delivery (NAILDD) Project to improve the quality and cost effectiveness of interlibrary loan and document delivery. The genesis and overall scope of this initiative is described elsewhere in this volume. This chapter discusses issues of system architecture and technological infrastructure that will be needed to support the effort, with particular attention to those areas where organizational decisions will drive choices about architecture. It also covers some of the standards and interoperability problems that must be addressed to make the initiative a success.

The driving forces for the NAILDD initiative have to do with

Clifford A. Lynch is Director of Library Automation at the University of California in Oakland, CA.

[Haworth co-indexing entry note]: "System Architecture and Networking Issues in Implementing the North American Interlibrary Loan and Document Delivery (NAILDD) Initiative." Lynch, Clifford A. Co-published simultaneously in *Journal of Library Administration* (The Haworth Press, Inc.) Vol. 21, No. 1/2, 1995, pp. 145-167; and *The Future of Resource Sharing* (ed: Shirley K. Baker, and Mary E. Jackson) The Haworth Press, Inc., 1995, pp. 145-167. Multiple copies of this article/chapter may be purchased from The Haworth Document Delivery Center [1-800-342-9678; 9:00 a.m. - 5:00 p.m. (EST)].

© 1995 by The Haworth Press, Inc. All rights reserved.   *145*

146 THE FUTURE OF RESOURCE SHARING

controlling costs and improving service to library patrons in an environment where escalating costs limit any given library to holding an ever-diminishing portion of the published literature, and thus require libraries to function as an increasingly interdependent national and even international system rather than independent, self-sufficient organizations. As well as being driven from service and economic imperatives, the NAILDD program exploits new opportunities that have been created as a result of investments in technology over the last two decades. In particular:

1. Major research libraries throughout North America are now connected by the Internet, a neutral and increasingly ubiquitous computer communications network (unlike earlier, proprietary networks, where a political or business alignment was a condition of connectivity, and competing networks were not interconnected with each other) which should facilitate resource sharing and document delivery processes. In addition, commercial document supply services and publishers are increasingly connected to the Internet as well, allowing them to interact more easily with libraries via electronic systems, and making the document delivery and interlibrary loan processes increasingly similar. Finally, libraries and their end users are also linked by the Internet, facilitating the identification, requesting, and delivery of information from library to patron. The Internet provides a global context for commerce among libraries, their suppliers, and their clients.

2. Information about the holdings of libraries has increasingly become accessible in electronic databases through investments in local integrated online library systems (IOLS), regional online catalogs, and participation in international services like OCLC and RLIN, combined with progress in retrospective conversion efforts. The availability of these databases on the Internet, in a form increasingly suitable for programs as well as humans to access through protocols like Z39.50, greatly facilitates the automatic routing of interlibrary loan requests. (The Z39.50 protocol allows *programs* at one site to conduct searches of remote catalogs in support of interlibrary loan processes and to retrieve search results that are in a form suitable for subsequent postprocessing by these same programs.) Access to these resources is typically free, except for the

international services like OCLC and RLIN, and even here, too, costs of access are dropping steadily.

3. Patrons identify, locate, and select more and more material through online catalogs and network-accessible abstracting and indexing databases, thus enabling the capture of accurate and complete descriptions of desired material at the point of request. Further, because of the growth of applications based on protocols such as Z39.50, which interchange structured records, data elements in these materials descriptions are increasingly machine-parseable, which means that they can be analyzed by automated systems and, where appropriate, be routed automatically to ILL/document delivery systems. Current standards development efforts, including document ordering through Z39.50 version 3 extended services and the efforts of NISO (the National Information Standards Organization) to develop a downloading standard for bibliographic and A&I records suitable for use in terminal emulation environments, will further increase the availability of materials requests in structured formats that include key bibliographic data elements.

4. Libraries are beginning to use automated systems communicating across the network to transact business with other libraries and with library suppliers of all types. Electronic data interchange (EDI) transactions among libraries, publishers, and document supply services are becoming commonplace, making commercial transactions among automated systems on the network routine and leading to the establishment of local organizational policies (including business and finance policies) that facilitate network-based commerce; in this connection it is important to recognize that organizational acceptance of network-based commercial transactions are much more than a technical issue. International standards (ISO 10160 and 10161) have also been established for the network-based interchange and processing of interlibrary loan requests among libraries. These standards have also been extended to include document ordering and have been, to some degree, linked with version 3 of the Z39.50 information retrieval protocol through the extended services facility in Z39.50. Patron record data elements are being defined that will allow groups of libraries to authenticate patrons reciprocally for borrowing purposes.

Despite these enabling developments, achieving the objectives of

148   THE FUTURE OF RESOURCE SHARING

the NAILDD Project will be a tremendously challenging technological feat. It will require an unprecedented degree of integration
among disparate, autonomously managed, and independently developed (by competing vendors) library automation systems. It will
require a more serious and rigorous implementation of standards,
with an emphasis on broad-based interoperability among systems,
than is now typical in libraries or library automation systems in
order to achieve the requisite levels of interoperability on a large
scale. The problem here is not just vendor implementations, but
local decisions about options, customization, and practices. To cite
only one example, it will be necessary to exchange effectively
serials holding information through protocols like Z39.50. And it
will require that participating libraries place a much greater premium on the ability to cooperate with each other effectively, even if
this takes place at the expense of the library's continued ability to
implement complex and perhaps slightly idiosyncratic practices that
are finely tuned to the needs of its local constituency. Finally, it will
demand a consensus on a model (or at most a small set of models)
of the resource sharing environment.

The NAILDD initiative will unfold against the context of a rapidly changing environment that is going to get much more complex
and uncertain than today's primarily print-based world. At least in
my view, the heart of the NAILDD initiative is to improve libraries'
ability to deliver material to patrons by targeting all aspects of the
traditional interlibrary loan process of obtaining materials on behalf
of library users, while recognizing that one option for improving
this process is to acquire materials from commercial document
supply services as well as from other libraries. NAILDD is about
supplying *print* more efficiently (including using information
technology such as facsimile transmission, including network-
based fax transmission, to deliver printed copy) and, as such, operates within the broad legal and commercial framework that has
traditionally governed the delivery of print materials from library to
library—the CONTU guidelines and related interlibrary loan practices, copyright law, the doctrine of first sale, and fair use rights.
There is growing evidence, at least in my view, that the highest
payoff for NAILDD may be in routing requests efficiently rather
than in exploiting information technology and computer-commu-

nications networks for improved delivery of material; however, since the tightening interpretations of copyright law that are developing in the networked information environment are suggesting that some uses of information technology to improve delivery via electronic transmission may be restricted and thus only available to libraries by paying a substantial premium, both in fees to rightsholders and in overhead in determining what fees are needed and where and how to pay them.

At the same time that the NAILDD initiative is proceeding, a much more massive and wide-reaching set of changes is overtaking the library community (and indeed challenging the basic traditional institutional roles of libraries) as published materials that have traditionally appeared in print migrate into electronic form and legal and commercial arrangements controlling the acquisition and use of this material move from a framework defined by public policy, sale, and copyright to one defined by license agreements under contract law, or, if still governed by the copyright framework, a new copyright framework, into the potentially very restrictive interpretations of copyright proposed by groups such as the Information Infrastructure Task Force (IITF) Committee on Intellectual Property in the National Information Infrastructure (NII) chaired by Bruce Lehman. As a counterpoint to this increasingly restrictive usage framework surrounding traditional publishing as it moves to the networked environment, much scholarly communication is moving into networked-based channels that are not controlled by traditional publishers; rather, distribution of information through these new channels operates under the control of individual authors or under the auspices of organizations such as professional societies that do not (or at least should not) have a profit-making motivation. These developments in the system of scholarly communication are disintermediating libraries from their traditional roles in the scholarly communications process as well. In the long term, these developments will probably limit the impact of the potential achievements of the NAILDD initiatives—but will not render them irrelevant or even insignificant, since in my view we will continue to operate in a mixed print and electronic environment for decades to come—and will demand a much more fundamental rethinking of how libraries satisfy the information requirements of their patrons. The implications of this transition of scholarly publishing to the networked information environment are, however, beyond the scope of this chapter.

MODELS AND ARCHITECTURES FOR NORTH AMERICAN RESOURCE SHARING

We first consider the "wide-area" problems involved in the NAILDD initiative. Institutions generate requests for materials that they need for their patrons but are unable to supply locally. (The generation of these requests is considered later in this chapter.) Each library defines policies for targeting sources of supply for these requests. There are a number of complex criteria that go into the targeting process, including the speed with which the needed material can be supplied, the existence of cooperative agreements among lending and borrowing libraries (perhaps supported by special, expedited transportation arrangements), the fee that the lending library will assess to the borrowing institution or other costs of acquiring the materials for the patron, and other factors. A mix of automated processes and human analysis by interlibrary loan librarians is used to match requests to suppliers within the broad framework of the originating library's targeting policy. The policy—and particularly the degree to which a given library wants to focus interlibrary loan activity on a specific set of partner libraries and document supply services, rather than assigning requests broadly on a national and international basis—will dictate the most efficient technical methods for implementing the routing of interlibrary loan or document acquisition requests.

There are also policy choices involved in selecting the *means* of identifying *potential* lenders for interlibrary loan. These may include a decision to select only institutions that offer direct Z39.50 access to their own local catalog databases, thus permitting the borrowing institution to avoid fees for using an ILL management and routing system offered by a central organization like OCLC. These choices are distinct from the influence of possible borrowing charges in the ultimate selection of a target lender from the set of prospective lenders.

There is a wide range of feasible system architectures to support

NAILDD. At one extreme, one can consider a centralized system such as OCLC's ILL offering. Here candidate lenders holding the requisite material are identified through searching a central union catalog database, and then ranked in priority order according to criteria defined by the borrowing library (including loan fees, geographic proximity, participation in regional or other consortia). The use of such centralized systems and the emphasis on traditional interlibrary loan rather than document acquisition on demand have been the most common practice historically for most libraries.

At the other extreme one can envision fully distributed systems in which the borrowing library sequentially probes local catalogs at various institutions to identify *potential* lending libraries based on a ranking algorithm defined at the borrowing library. Such an algorithm is likely to be quite complex; it may be locally developed, and at the very least will be extensively parameterized and tuned to meet a given borrowing institution's needs. The algorithm may also include a learning component that considers historical performance data gathered from the results of previous requests sent to various suppliers. A successful probe might be followed immediately by an ILL request, or the probing process may continue for some time to identify a set of candidate suppliers, and then a second stage of the ranking algorithm might be used to select a "best" potential supplier from the candidate supplier pool. Identifying even a single potential supplier meeting the borrowing library's policy constraints may require a large number of probes. While multiple probes could be carried out in parallel, the complexity and added cost of doing this is probably unnecessary; each probe will take a matter of a few tens of seconds at most. Even if many sites need to be probed, parallel queries will not save more than a few minutes in the generation of an ILL request, and these few minutes will be saved at the cost of considerable technical complexity and additional search processing at both the borrowing site and the sites that it is probing. The Z39.50 computer-to-computer information retrieval protocol is the key technology that makes this type of distributed probing possible.

Hybrid solutions are possible based on regional union catalogs for local library consortia. These regional union catalogs are searched first, followed, if necessary, by consultation of either indi-

152   *THE FUTURE OF RESOURCE SHARING*

vidual library online catalogs outside of the local consortium or national level databases such as OCLC to identify targets for requests that cannot be satisfied within the local consortium. If a regional union catalog is used to identify potential lending sites, it may still be necessary to consult the local catalog at a specific site that is a participant in the regional union catalog site to determine if the material required is expected to be on the shelf or if it is known to be out on loan, or to check details of serials holdings.

From a technology perspective, the more that the originating library wants to consult potential suppliers directly rather than operating purely through some type of central "broker" system like OCLC, the more important standards become, because more and more unfamiliar autonomous systems need to be able to communicate with each other. In the case of a single centralized system, standards per se really matter very little; the local system at the requesting library must simply be able to communicate with the central system, if necessary using proprietary interfaces defined by the central system. Put another way, the centralized system sets a de facto standard which local IOLSs must implement. (If there are multiple competing central systems, then standards for interfaces become a bit more of an issue since these facilitate the ability of a requesting library to use multiple central systems concurrently, or to switch allegiance from one to another easily. But as long as there are only a small number of central systems, their interfaces can still be viewed as de facto standards–the extent to which these standards are the same will result in natural cost savings. Conformance to such a de facto standard is very clear and readily tested; a specific local IOLS either can or cannot communicate successfully with the central system.) A purchaser of a local IOLS system only has to verify interoperability with one or at most a few centralized systems, and if the IOLS system doesn't interoperate successfully, there is typically a presumption that the IOLS vendor is at fault, since the centralized system establishes a de facto standard that is in essence defined by its behavior. In contrast, if a local IOLS system is expected to communicate successfully with a vast array of other IOLS systems, it is necessary to rely on an open standard and the verification of conformance to this standard (or, more to the point, the assignment of blame and responsibility for fixing software) is a much more complex and murky issue.

A centralized system also serves as a repository for a robust and well-tested set of algorithms for selecting potential suppliers of material. In this sense it protects all participating libraries from "rogue" erroneous supplier selection algorithms that may be put into operation accidentally at a borrowing library and which may cause immense amounts of network traffic and queries against remote systems.

To accomplish the NAILDD objectives, the character of the interfaces to a central source must expand to allow direct queries from local IOLS systems, not merely queries constructed interactively by ILL librarians at borrowing libraries. A central site must incorporate good programmatic interfaces that allow requests to be routed automatically from a library's local system to the central ILL management system.

Another architectural issue implicit in the extremes that have just been described is whether the borrower wants to take the strategy of locating candidate sites that are *known* to have the material *prior* to issuing a request to borrow (thus placing the onus on the recipient of the request to reject that request if it does not want to loan to the potential borrower); or whether the borrower wants to do a more sophisticated screening that considers not only what materials are available at the target sites but also published information about their policies. At the other extreme, a choice needs to be made as to whether the borrowing site simply wants to route broadly a request to borrow materials, leaving it to the sites receiving the request to determine whether they even have the material in question as well as whether they are willing to loan it.

Both of these architectural models are relatively static, in the sense that the ranking of candidate sites takes place statically at the borrowing library (or within a central routing system acting as a proxy for the borrowing library) according to a set of policy constraints (geography, proximity, delay, infrastructure, and cost), and libraries generally transact with a well-established and well-known set of partners. Costs for borrowing material are assumed to be essentially fixed for each supplier, at least over relatively long periods of time—months or even years. There is no real competition among suppliers. Choice is driven largely by the way the borrower routes probes and/or requests (depending on whether the borrower checks availability before asking for material to be loaned). Further, the emphasis is typically on routing interlibrary loan requests to other libraries rather than to document supply services, so price competition is less of a factor.

There is also a third model that is becoming at least potentially feasible (though still, realistically, somewhat beyond the capabilities of the installed technology base or the operational practices of existing organizations that comprise the ILL system) based on marketplace auction models. Here, *for each transaction,* the borrowing library would submit a request for bids (including in the request information such as how quickly the material is needed) from potential lenders or suppliers across the network, and organizations which could supply the needed material would respond to the borrower with bids that included terms and conditions such as cost and time to supply. After some period of time during which these electronic bids arrive, the source library would select a supplier and award the contract to supply the material.

This auction marketplace model is characterized by a much broader and more variable set of suppliers for materials and by an emphasis purely on cost and quality of service rather than on inter-organizational arrangements and alliances or similar static policies. To really exploit the possible advantages of such a bidding environment, however, requires new thinking and much greater agility on the part of the participants. To be most effective, for example, it would require supplying organizations to set prices dynamically depending on how busy they are with requests and what resources they currently have available to service external interlibrary loan requests and based on an understanding of their costs to satisfy requests, and not just to quote a fixed price based on a role as regional or national supplier of last resort without regard to quality of service parameters. A supplier might change price quotes for supplying a given article several times per day, based on the number of requests that it had accepted for fulfillment already that day. Libraries awarding delivery "contracts" would also need to track performance of suppliers over time (presumably through automated systems, since the assumption is that most bids would be awarded entirely through analysis by computer programs on the local system and computer-computer transactions). A robust system would need to filter out bids from suppliers that frequently promise more than they can really deliver.

From an implementation perspective, such a marketplace could be either completely distributed (with bids issued through some form of reliable multicast service on the Internet–which, it should be noted, does not really exist today, although the foundations in IP multicast technology do exist, and are being used for other applications), or centralized (with some organization or *organizations* operating a marketplace to which bids are centrally submitted and then rerouted to potential suppliers). The local institutional systems needed–both at the borrower and supplier sites–to originate, evaluate, select among, and respond to such bids for document supply do not exist today, nor do the requisite standards (though the current interlibrary loan protocol could provide a probable point of departure in developing such a system). The models that might guide the development of such a market auction based environment include automated stock, commodity and financial exchanges; the policy and regulatory, as well as technical issues that surround such exchanges give a sense of the complexity of such a market auction environment. Consider the details of implementing such simple-sounding concepts as "awarding a contract" to a supplier in this environment. Are there notions of public promises of performance, or of binding legal agreements? Can one potential supplier see the bids of other potential suppliers in response to a request from a borrowing institution?

Does the dynamic auction market model make sense? Certainly, it is much more intensive in its use of, and hence need for, investment in information technology and networks than today's systems. If some institutions want to loan, making profit from supplying materials, and others make loans only reluctantly in their role as suppliers of last resort (as part of a broader policy commitment to participation in the research library community nationally and internationally, for example), then it may have some benefits. It has the strengths that encourage price competition, and it permits suppliers to vary their policies, sometimes encouraging borrowing and sometimes discouraging it through economic controls. To the extent that supplying organizations want to alternate between inviting and discouraging requests (for example, to smooth staffing in the face of variable local demand), it offers real advantages. It does assume that the computational costs of operating the marketplace are much smaller than the charges for the actual document supply transaction once the partners in this transaction are identified through the auction market. Also, we know from other auction marketplaces (such as the stock and commodities markets) that stability within such a marketplace is very complex to achieve; one can imagine participants facing substantial price volatility that might have to be managed through schemes like trading in futures and derivatives. I am not optimistic that the typical ILL department will cope with this well, or that the typical future IOLS system will support the demands of such an environment very effectively; the auction marketplace offers increased economic efficiency and flexibility at the cost of tremendously increased complexity and volatility.

The choice of appropriate architecture is as much economic as it is technical. From a purely technical basis, use of a single highly centralized system would seem to be extremely efficient and cost effective, particularly if extended to include commercial document supply services as well as libraries. But some libraries want to avoid paying to place their holdings in a centralized system (thus allowing other libraries to consider them as suppliers) or paying to search against a national union database (that might include holdings of commercial document supply services as well as other libraries) as part of the borrowing process. Some libraries arguing against the costs of a central service may be confusing explicit costs—in the sense of real dollars flowing out of an institution to an international utility like OCLC—with much harder-to-identify costs for networks, local systems, intersystem searching, and staff.

It is difficult to really assess the economic implications of these architectural choices, since the costs for using central system approaches like OCLC tend to be well-specified, but the costs of establishing and searching regional union catalogs, or of sequentially searching a set of local catalogs and then transmitting a request from one local system to another are generally not well-identified, and indeed are very hard to conclusively establish. We also don't have a good grasp on the economic cost of system failures of various kinds–failure to locate potential borrowers, forcing human intervention and review of a request for materials, misrouting of requests to inappropriate borrowers, etc. It seems likely that at least in the near term centralized systems will be less prone to errors; they are simpler and more predictable. They are also much easier to maintain.

Any central system is in some sense a monopoly; it is hard for a competitor to enter the marketplace due to the need to obtain a database of holdings information upon which to base routing decisions. And, to an extent, competition does not serve the user community well as it is likely to further fragment coverage of holdings databases and reduce the effectiveness of all routing systems in operation. This raises the specter of uncontrollable price escalation by the monopoly central system operator. If, as in the case of OCLC, this central system operator is a not-for-profit that is essentially owned and governed by the user community, there are at least checks and balances to control such price escalation. But this is also ultimately an argument for long-term consideration of the auction market model.

There is also a political dimension to the acceptance of central systems. Some libraries simply don't like or distrust such enormous central systems; they are concerned that they will become costly and unresponsive. There are concerns that simply because such a system represents a natural means of assigning charges to ILL lending that its existence may be undesirable; the argument here is that the policy of charging for loans is so strongly to be avoided that it is an argument against setting up any system that could provide a mechanism to support such a recharge policy. In other cases, there is, I believe, a view that politically ILL routing should be handled at a state or consortium level, providing roles (and perhaps revenue streams) for a multiplicity of smaller, less efficient (in terms of holdings coverage and thus probability of being able to route the maximum number of requests successfully) routing systems. While many of these concerns may have some real legitimacy, I believe that one of the challenges of the NAILDD initiative is to move beyond these concerns as barriers to progress and increased overall efficiency of the North American ILL and document delivery system.

158   THE FUTURE OF RESOURCE SHARING

No centralized system exists today that incorporates the holdings of all potential supplier libraries, much less the additional offerings of all document supply services. Perhaps the most comprehensive is OCLC's system (the scope of which is likely to be further extended as it is gatewayed to other ILL systems), but for some requests libraries will still have to go outside of this system, by routing their requests to other systems or suppliers (perhaps after considerable research by the local library's ILL unit). Thus most large libraries will be quick to point out that for the foreseeable future no single system will meet all of their needs to obtain materials for their patrons. But I believe that at least until the technical infrastructure to support implementation of a market auction model, and more importantly, a consensus that this extra complexity will be beneficial, emerges, that from a technical and economic basis, the library community will likely be well-served by maximizing use of a central routing system.

SETTLEMENTS AND FINANCIAL ISSUES

When I first became involved in discussions about the NAILDD Project, I was stunned to discover that interlibrary loan participants actually wrote substantial numbers of small checks to each other. The borrowing institution wrote a check for a few dollars to the lender, mailed the lender the check, and then the lender deposited it. The overhead costs for these transactions must be staggering. I am convinced that the participants have no firm, rigorously supportable data about their overhead costs, either to generate or to receive a payment; but I am certain that in cases where an institution either generates or receives payments of the size under discussion the overhead to write the check and mail it is larger than the amount of the check; further, the institution *receiving* the check probably loses money as well. This process of settlements for ILL fees is an obvious candidate for high-payoff automation; but automating this process is not simple, as it involves the business processes, procedures and policies of both participating institutions in a fundamental way, as well as technical considerations.

It is important to be clear what process is to be automated. One approach is to simply replace the transmission of a paper check with an electronic transaction. The computer at the lending institution sends the computer at the borrowing institution a bill; the borrowing institution tells its bank to transmit payment to the bank that services the lending institution as a means of paying that bill. This will certainly reduce costs, but because of the banks involved there will still be substantial electronic funds transfer costs involved which may well dominate the value of the actual funds being interchanged. The major issues here are technical–setting up the appropriate electronic data interchange (EDI) links among institutions and banks; integrating support for generating the appropriate EDI transactions into the local systems of the participating libraries (and the central routing system, if there is one); and to a lesser extent procedural in that the electronic funds transfer practices need to be brought into conformance with the business and finance policies at each participating institution.

A second approach would be to have each institution maintain balances owed to other institutions; once every quarter, or annually, funds would actually be transferred, either by writing paper checks or by electronic funds transfer. This is much more complex than the first objective. While it is likely that there will be many small transactions (between pairs of institutions that don't do much business with each other, and where again the overhead costs of the electronic transactions may be as large as the amounts being transferred, as in the first case), substantial amounts of money may move in a single transaction between some pairs of libraries. Thus, issues of credit-worthiness, auditability, interest on funds owed, and even currency value fluctuations (among partners in different nations) arise as serious issues in establishing such a system.

A third, even more ambitious, goal would be to establish what is in essence a special-purpose "central bank" for settling accounts among all participants in the ILL fabric.

Periodically, each participant would either transfer funds to, or receive funds from, the central clearinghouse. This would have the advantage of minimizing the number of actual funds transfers and the overhead associated with them. The central clearinghouse would deal with all of the problems of extending credit, currency exchange, and the like. It is unclear to me what sorts of business and finance policy questions the participating organizations would raise

160 *THE FUTURE OF RESOURCE SHARING*

with regard to auditability of the actions of the central clearing-house, but the advantage would be that these issues would have to be addressed with only one external organization rather than a vast range of trading partners within the broad North American ILL system.

In the centralized model where an organization like OCLC runs an interlibrary loan routing and requesting system the utility could easily do billing periodically and act as a central payments clearing-house; indeed, this seems to be simpler than trying to implement the first two of the three alternatives for financial settlements described above. In the context of a central routing system for ILL, the clear-inghouse function is straightforward and likely minimizes interaction with local business and finance policies at any of the participating institutions. It is incomprehensible to me why this wasn't done years ago. It is also worth noting that this clearinghouse can offer very significant benefits without the requirement that libraries be capable of supporting EDI transactions. Since each participating institution only writes or receives one check per period (say per quarter) the costs of writing or depositing the checks are not very significant. Such a central clearinghouse could do EDI transactions for those institutions which could support them, and write checks or bills for the institutions that cannot today support EDI.

In distributed models of ILL, a clearinghouse function for pay-ments is enormously more difficult. All transactions would have to be reported to the clearinghouse, with appropriate security, authen-tication and auditability considerations being taken into account. It is unclear just what regulatory issues would arise in the operation of such a clearinghouse, particularly on an international basis.

The first two financial scenarios are slightly easier to implement in that they just require peer institution EDI exchanges rather than the existence of a central clearinghouse to which transactions are reported, but they are still very complex. Virtually all of the partici-pants in the system would have to be EDI capable for efficiencies to be gained, and they would have to support EDI with the most demanding type of interoperability–being able to communicate not just with a well known central clearinghouse but with a very large number of peer institutions on a relatively casual basis. And all of the business and financial policy and practice issues at an institutional level will have to be addressed at each participating institution.

In all situations it is worth noting that EDI transactions are not currently well integrated with the ILL protocol (ISO 10160 and 10161) so substantial standards development work would likely be needed. A central system, with its ability to set de facto standards, might well lead to more rapid implementation progress.

The extension of such a payments settlement system to document suppliers as well as libraries does not introduce too much which is new. The major new complication is the possible need to collect sales tax, and to determine in what jurisdiction a transaction occurred, particularly given the existence of proxy agents that may reroute requests.

Many institutions are developing policies that reflect some or all of the cost of using a document delivery service (or sometimes even of ILL borrowing) back to the end user or the end user's department or other organizational unit in at least some circumstances. This adds some very substantial complexity to the implementation of a payment settlements system. On one side it may introduce the requirement that document suppliers or local library systems at supplier libraries be able to bill charges via credit card systems; here the borrowing library would include the patron's credit card information with the document request. Credit card billing is not conceptually difficult (and is supported today by most commercial document supply services) but will be a new issue for most supplier libraries, who may try to push the problem back to requesting libraries by arguing that the borrowing library should bill the credit card, and that the lending library wants to maintain its relationships with borrowing libraries rather than patrons at the borrowing library directly. This assignment of responsibility, it seems likely, will be argued to be analogous to the borrowing library's assumption of responsibility for the action of its patrons in the handling and return of returnable materials obtained via ILL.

The other side is that interfaces to institutional debit card or other accounting systems may be needed. As charges are reported by systems at the lending library, some or all of these charges will be recharged to some type of local financial system at the borrowing library (be it a pure accounting system, as for departmental funds,

162 *THE FUTURE OF RESOURCE SHARING*

or something like a debit card system). Today, all such interfaces are, to the best of my knowledge, custom-designed. As a rule, local IOLS systems do not support such interfaces; nor do they contain provisions for algorithmic, rule-based splitting and partial reassignment of charges that arrive from remote systems via EDI or ILL transactions. Standards in this area are likely to be very far off, since institutional accounting systems are among the most idiosyncratic electronic information systems at any institution, and they are deeply embedded in the financial and business policies and procedures of an institution. This is an area where considerable custom local development will be needed to realize the full NAILDD vision.

THE BORROWING LIBRARY PERSPECTIVE: ORIGINATION AND INITIAL ROUTING OF DOCUMENT REQUESTS

Consider the perspective of a library patron. Perhaps the simplest case is where he or she has located some desired material by searching an abstracting and indexing (A&I) database located on the "home" system, or by filling out a blank order screen (in the situation where he or she wants a book that isn't in the local catalog, or an article that he or she cannot find in any of the local A&I databases). The local library automation system will need to determine whether the request for materials can be satisfied by local holdings; this may involve examination of the linkage between serials holdings and A&I database, or it may involve an attempt to match a citation for a book or journal article against a local monographic or serials catalog. For serials, detailed holdings will likely need to be considered. For monographs (and perhaps serials, depending on local circulation policies) circulation status of materials may also have to be checked to see if the material is believed to be on the shelf. If the system is unable to make an automated match, the first policy question is whether the library is prepared to route the request for ILL processing or whether it feels the need to perform a costly manual review to make certain that the material isn't held locally. Part of the ideal underlying the NAILDD initiative is that such manual review should be avoided as a costly, needless delay, assuming that the automated system can make the determination with a fairly high degree of accuracy. The ability to perform this check effectively has wide reaching implications for the importance of accurate data elements to permit A&I databases to be linked to serials holdings, and for the importance of good matching algorithms for citations. Other local policies and strategies come into play here as well: whether to recall materials locally to satisfy a request, or to send the request on to ILL because it cannot be quickly satisfied locally. In some cases, where the library is pursuing an explicit access vs. ownership strategy, certain materials may automatically be routed to ILL or document supply with a special indication that the library will pay all costs of filling the request. In other cases, cost allocation decisions may be made based on the degree of delivery urgency indicated in the user's request and the various sources that the material can be obtained from (and the costs of employing these various sources).

It is important to recognize how much extra complexity parameters that the user supplies in requesting material can add. To take one example, the assumption has traditionally been that users want paper copies of materials. In an age of increasingly commonplace personal databases, a user may well ask for an article in ASCII format, indicating that a print copy or a bitmapped image is unacceptable for his or her purposes. Or consider the case of urgent delivery. In some cases, such as journals published abroad, citations to articles may appear in A&I databases long before the printed journal reaches the library shelves; rapid delivery of this material would require specialized document supply services (probably at a premium price). As another example, some libraries license fulltext databases, but the appearance of articles in these fulltext databases may lag print publication by a month or more due to publisher embargoes and/or processing delays for scanning or offshore rekeyboarding of articles. Here again the library must recognize complex supply parameters and cost tradeoffs.

More and more, however, the user isn't simply searching local databases for material. He or she may identify material by searching online catalogs throughout the Internet, or licensed databases mounted at sites remote from the local library (either because the local library has licensed access to these A&I databases for its user community or is participating in some kind of consortium access arrangement, or even because the patron is paying directly to search these databases commercially). In these situations the patron must decide whether to act independently of his or her "home" institution and to pay directly for documents. Alternatively, the patron can route requests back through the "home" local system for processing, thus perhaps gaining access to some financial subsidy or special pricing that his or her local library offers for supplying material (whether held locally at the home institution, or acquired by ILL or document delivery by the home library), in which case they may receive a partial or complete subsidy. Currently, transmission of the request back to the home system, if the patron chooses to take this route, is awkward, involving cut and paste operations into an order form at the local system (using the patron's workstation as a simultaneous window into two systems, the local and the remote, which cannot communicate directly with each other) or the transmission of an electronic mail request; standards and protocols are not yet in place to transmit a structured, machine-parseable citation to a home system for ordering. These problems decrease the probability that the home system, upon receiving the request, can do an accurate match to local holdings, and thus make a good decision (without manual review) about whether to attempt to fill the request from local resources or reroute it through ILL/document delivery services. These increasingly commonplace service scenarios suggest that improvements in the ability of users to initiate such intersystem document delivery requests should be a high priority in the development of intersystem protocols and data interchange standards.

THE LAST MILE: RESPONSIBILITIES FOR DELIVERY TO THE PATRON

A final architectural issue is how material reaches the patron that asked for it. This has been a question even in the print environment, particularly for non-returnable items: should the lending (or, more generally, supplying) institution mail the material directly to the patron, or send it to the borrowing library which will then take responsibility for getting it to the patron (either through campus mail, or by holding it for pickup by the patron at the library). The obvious advantage of sending to the borrowing library is that the borrowing library can track the completion of the document request on behalf of its patron (and also gather performance statistics); the obvious disadvantage is additional delay in getting the material into the patron's hands. Of course, for returnable items, it is more important that the borrowing library verify receipt of material that it must take responsibility for returning in good order.

In the electronic delivery environment matters become more complicated. The amount of delay that is introduced by routing requested material back through the borrowing (or more generally, ordering) library may be a matter of at most a few minutes, if appropriate automated systems are in place to acknowledge receipt of the material and automatically reroute it on to the patron for final delivery. If manual intervention is involved, the delay introduced by this step may dominate the time for the entire delivery process and thus may have a major effect on the quality of service to the patron. Very few local systems today can support the necessary receipt and forwarding operations automatically, however.

There are also some substantial technical arguments for "buffering" the received material at the borrowing library. An end user's workstation may not be powered on when the requested material arrives. Or the user may not understand that a rather large amount of disk space will be needed to hold a 50 page article in bitmapped image form, as it might be received by some network fax or ARIEL-type delivery mechanism; an attempt to deliver direct to the patron might fail because the necessary resources aren't available. The user may really want a printed copy, and may not have a high quality printer available to print the requisite material. Or, to take yet another example, the patron may be at home on the end of a very slow 14.4 Kbit/second link; while the borrowing library may be accessible through a very fast link on the Internet and capable of receiving a large document from the lending library in a matter of a minute or less, it could take hours for the lending library to transmit the document directly to the requesting patron. Depending on how the lending library has designed its transmission facilities for documents (and, in particular, the number of requests that it can be fulfilling in parallel), a large number of other document transmission requests may be queued behind the transmission to the patron on the slow link.

In my view, the borrowing library should typically receive materials from the lending library or document supplier and buffer them for the patron. This has several implications. The borrowing library needs to be able to receive documents quickly; it needs transient storage space to house large amounts of material; and it needs to be able to automatically associate incoming documents with requests from patrons within its users' community, and to forward them on to the patron automatically and quickly. This again calls for substantial development in local systems, and integration between document ordering/borrowing facilities and document delivery facilities.

CONCLUSION

Several points are clear from this analysis of architectural alternatives to support the NAILDD Project. A great deal of development is going to be needed at the local IOLS level. A new type of system component, where a local library defines (and subsequently maintains and refines) rules or algorithms at a high level rather than writing code, is going to be needed. These IOLS systems will have to support a much broader range of interfaces to external systems, which will include ILL/document supply routing, EDI, queries against external databases, document requesting, and checking and forwarding of documents from external systems.

Standards and their implementation will be a key part of the NAILDD environment. To the extent that this environment is fully distributed, rather than a set of local, in-library systems communicating with one or at most a few centralized international routing and management systems, standards conformance and interoperability issues will become both central and extremely challenging.

This chapter has not addressed statistics and management data directly; yet the collection and reporting of this data will also be a central component of an effective implementation of the NAILDD vision. Management data collection and reporting is a highly customized function, much like the linkages to local accounting systems discussed earlier. Yet it is an essential function, and one that cannot be overlooked.

In considering system architectures to support the NAILDD initiative, there is a great tendency to favor fully distributed approaches that do not have any central routing function. As this chapter illustrates, such implementation approaches are certainly feasible, but they are extremely challenging both from a technical and a policy perspective. One of the major questions that we must consider as we plan the implementation of the NAILDD vision is the extent to which we wish to deal with these very real complexities as a price for the perceived philosophical and political benefits of the fully distributed environment. While in the long term these may offer the most flexible models, in the near term it may be much easier and more practical to make progress within a framework of more centralized implementations.

The Future of Document Delivery: A Vendor's Perspective

Melissa Stockton
Martha Whittaker

Much has been written lately in the library press about the future of scholarly publishing, the future of interlibrary loan, and the future of the library in general. In the library and publishing worlds, two groups that have always viewed each other rather cautiously, electronic publishing is commanding everyone's interest. Particular attention is being paid to the ways in which electronic publishing will alter the traditional relationship of library to publisher. This comes at a time when the popular media have discovered their newest "hot item"–the information superhighway.

It is within this context that this paper addresses the future of document delivery from a vendor's viewpoint, and how the coalescence of interlibrary loan, electronic information sources, and document delivery is altering their relationships to one another. The article focuses primarily on the document delivery vendors who are themselves "wired," offering online access to locating tools, usually designed for unmediated searching and ordering. It is assumed that all these vendors support some form of electronic delivery of the articles.

Melissa Stockton is Product Specialist with the UnCover Company in Denver, CO.

Martha Whittaker is General Manager with the UnCover Company in Denver, CO.

[Haworth co-indexing entry note]: "The Future of Document Delivery: A Vendor's Perspective." Stockton, Melissa, and Martha Whittaker. Co-published simultaneously in *Journal of Library Administration* (The Haworth Press, Inc.) Vol. 21, No. 1/2, 1995, pp. 169-181; and *The Future of Resource Sharing* (ed: Shirley K. Baker, and Mary E. Jackson) The Haworth Press, Inc., 1995, pp. 169-181. Multiple copies of this article/chapter may be purchased from The Haworth Document Delivery Center [1-800-342-9678; 9:00 a.m. - 5:00 p.m. (EST)].

© 1995 by The Haworth Press, Inc. All rights reserved.

THE FUTURE OF RESOURCE SHARING

There is a trend toward referring to all interlibrary loan as document delivery, which indirectly recognizes that what libraries do falls within a subset of the larger universe of information delivery. The Internet, and specifically the commercialization of the Internet, has made information delivery an attractive industry for not just the large players–the Ameritechs, the Viacoms, and the Knight Ridders–but also the smaller niche market information providers, of which our company, the UnCover Company, is but one example.

One distinction that can be made between document delivery and interlibrary loan is in terms of material type. Books are loaned, almost always to be returned to the lending institution. Periodical articles, and to a lesser extent technical papers, annual reports and gray literature, are more commonly "delivered" permanently into the hands of the requester. Our focus in discussing the future of document delivery from a vendor's perspective is on this type of document delivery.

To a document delivery vendor, the deliverable is a product, in much the same way that to the publisher, the publication is the deliverable. The vendor's business revolves around selling the product, and while the vendor may be very conscious of the service performed, that service is designed to sell the product more efficiently (and profitably). Although the methods for providing good service may be similar to the library's methods, the vendor's motivation is likely to be somewhat less altruistic. A vendor develops a product with the market in mind, sells the product wherever the market exists, and develops and enhances the product with the cost/benefit model always in mind.

In looking to the future of document delivery, the vendor sees the same trends the library does, but may view them in a different way. In a very real sense, the document delivery provider is positioned between the publisher and the library–and dependent upon the goodwill of both. The document delivery vendor is arguably an intermediary, who might become irrelevant in the new world, where everyone has access to the network superhighway, and where everyone has all the needed computer power, bandwidth, and information packaging skills.

BETTER, FASTER, CHEAPER

Why use a document delivery vendor, anyway? The axiom of the marketing world is that in order for a product to succeed it must be better, faster, and cheaper.

Is a document delivery vendor better? Yes and no has to be the answer to this one. Articles made available through the UnCover service are cited in the UnCover database at approximately the same time as issues are received in libraries, making the currency of the service unparalleled. Most good vendors guarantee copyright compliance, freeing the library from the burden of tracking use and paying royalties. Many services offer "one-stop-shopping" which allows the librarian to send all requests to a single source without having to do the sometimes tedious work of locating owners one request at a time.

On the down side, electronic delivery of documents at times may offer a lesser quality image than the original or even a carefully photocopied and mailed reproduction. Additionally, the relative scarcity among commercial services of obscure or very old references makes them inappropriate for some purposes.

Are they faster? The answer to this one is almost always yes. In a carefully drawn study comparing a small sample of commercial document delivery sources to traditional interlibrary loan at Vassar College, authors Kurosman and Durniak found that the average time for an interlibrary loan request to arrive was 13 days.[1] Among commercial vendors with online indexes and fax or electronic delivery the average is usually in the 24 to 48 hour range. Both UnCover and UMI have a one hour service for certain categories of materials.

Is the vendor cheaper? In many cases the answer is yes. Even in the Vassar study, average cost per document (excluding overhead) ranged from under a dollar to over twenty dollars. Interlibrary loan was the lowest priced alternative. Nevertheless, the much cited ARL/RLG study of interlibrary loan costs found the aggregate costs of an average transaction to be $29.55.[2] This figure *does* include overhead, and also factors in the average costs both of lending and borrowing.

Until the ARL study, interlibrary loan departments in libraries have tended to ignore overhead and fixed costs. Libraries are not accustomed to operating as a business. "Costs" were considered to

172 *THE FUTURE OF RESOURCE SHARING*

be limited to payments required. By this somewhat unrealistic measurement, commercial document delivery is clearly not cheaper. Yet since there is stiff competition among document delivery vendors these days to keep per article costs in the $10-$15 range (once again not including the overhead that the library expends even when going to a vendor), most would conclude that when all factors are considered, document delivery vendors often are cheaper than the traditional library transaction.

Thus competitive pricing in document delivery benefits the consumer, as it does in many other areas. Competition among vendors is good for the user in both the price and service arena. Consumers of document delivery products tell us one thing: Keep it simple. While users want more sophisticated services, they also want pricing schema that are easy to understand and sell to management. When a variety of competing services are all priced approximately the same, what sets them apart is quite often the quality of the customer service they provide. Here again, competition works to the advantage of the consumer.

The market will pay where the value is taken. People will pay a premium for rapid delivery of materials if they are in time-sensitive situations, and won't if they aren't. They will pay for a database that is simple to use if it meets their needs the majority of the times they use it, and pay a premium for a database that is highly specialized, with sophisticated search options, when that is what they need.

COST/BENEFIT AND THE ROLE OF NETWORKS

There is no question that the future for document delivery is strong. As libraries experience dwindling resources, they will be forced to use their remaining assets wisely. Out of sheer necessity, libraries will be run more like businesses. Every library program, and every library purchase will be subjected to the same kind of cost/benefit analysis that is now common in the commercial sector. The idea of access to materials playing a major part of collection development policies is gaining acceptance, as the "just in time vs. just in case" concept of library ownership moves from a catchy phrase to a mainstream model, as libraries are no longer able to justify the purchase of expensive but little used materials. Far from being competitors, document delivery vendors view interlibrary loan as an important market for their services and in turn assist libraries by giving them what they need, when they need it.

Most libraries are now a part of a network and/or consortia. The first impulse in libraries, especially academic libraries, was to look toward each other as an answer to the ever-shrinking materials budgets with which they are faced. There are now regional library networks that allow libraries to access bibliographic sources such as OCLC and RLIN, as well as local consortia to provide vehicles for resource sharing among libraries in a specific area. The role that these networks consortia have played has changed as the needs of libraries have changed. The networks and consortia have had to develop new methods for aiding libraries as technology has changed. For example, many of the local networks which started as a means to access OCLC have branched out into other areas such as providing access to the Internet and group purchasing of high-dollar items such as online services, CD-ROMs, personal computers and local area network hardware. Many times opportunities not available to smaller libraries can be realized through the work of a consortium and libraries of all sizes can see a major cost efficiency when they join forces with other libraries in negotiating licensing fees or discounts from vendors.

Concurrent with these trends is the burgeoning of electronic resources and networking capabilities. The document delivery vendors have a new opportunity to use the information superhighway to provide their library clientele with far more sophisticated options for the access and acquisition of materials. Vendors help libraries, and their users, navigate through the seemingly overwhelming amount of sheer information, some valuable and some junk, on the network.

Virtually every major document supplier can be reached through the Internet. The larger vendors provide Telnet access to databases of the materials they offer. The best vendors provide some type of online ordering directly from the database–an online catalog more in the style of L.L. Bean than the library OPAC. Even the CD-ROM-based products, heretofore considered standalone or locally networkable products, are coming to the network. SilverPlatter's

174   *THE FUTURE OF RESOURCE SHARING*

new Electronic Reference Library offers Internet access to the SilverPlatter databases via its CD-ROM server.

The library of the future will be one vehicle for people to gain access to the world-wide information network. Both librarians and vendors will assume the role of mediator between this overwhelming amount of information and the patron who has a very specific information need. Few people will be able to navigate through the volume of information alone.

Sophisticated database searching software developed by commercial database providers and document delivery services is facilitating automated alert services. Both OCLC and UnCover have recently announced table of contents delivery services which will regularly send users TOCs from titles which they select from the companies' databases. The UnCover Reveal service allows users to order articles from these tables of contents by reply mail. Alert services based on subject interest areas and stored searches, similar to those available for years from companies such as Dialog, are the next step for document delivery vendors.

Libraries will retain those items of primary importance to their clientele. Libraries will rely on their own resource sharing partners (usually regional consortia) and document delivery vendors for items that are not used to a great extent. The consortia will only be an option to libraries if they have an existing system for document delivery similar to that offered by vendors.

Those users who have experience with going directly to document suppliers have high expectations for the delivery of documents. Online full text and 24-48 hour turnaround times for articles are becoming the standard, both for libraries and for vendors. The cost of being a part of the consortia and the turnaround time for articles are carefully considered by libraries before decisions are made as to where requests will be sent.

IMAGE DELIVERY

Every commercial vendor now offers delivery of TIFF (Tagged Image File Format) images to fax machines. Some are experimenting with FTP (File Transfer Protocol) image delivery to dedicated workstations. Document type definitions (DTDs) such as Acrobat, Folio, Replica and Common Ground will allow high quality viewing and printing of documents sent electronically. Increasingly common transport mechanisms such as MIME will enable e-mail delivery of images as well.

The most serious issue in image delivery is not technology, but copyright. Copyright concerns present a somewhat different challenge in the image delivery arena and the literature is replete with musings about the new copyright models required for the electronic distribution of intellectual property. That is not the subject of this paper; however, it is an issue of vital importance to the survival of document delivery, both from the vendor and from the library standpoint. While most publishers are reasonably comfortable with fax delivery–a kind of long-distance photocopy–the prospect of images flying around the networks on the kind of large scale that document delivery vendors are talking about is somewhat unsettling. Publishers have legitimate concerns with downstreaming, e.g., sending an image you've received on to 1000 of your closest friends, and with potential alteration of the data itself.

Ideas about the "new copyright paradigm" run all the way from the radical (copyright compliance can no longer be enforced, why try?) to the thoughtfully questioning (for example Ann Okerson's ideas on new models of ownership),[3] to the conservative (our present system can be adapted well with changes). The Copyright Clearance Center (CCC) has recently announced a new drive to secure electronic rights from publishers that contract with the CCC for royalty collection.[4]

The copyright issues notwithstanding, image delivery is nevertheless the wave of the future for document delivery. Fax-based delivery is presently the most popular alternative to mail, but this is because fax machines are nearly ubiquitous these days, and the high end workstation needed to receive and display compressed images is not nearly so prevalent yet. Depending on the size and speed of the line used to transmit images, it can take an unacceptable amount of time to get an article length file from sender to receiver. And images take a lot of storage space. The average office personal computer is not equipped to store multiple images, and campus-wide image servers are still primarily at the "pilot project" stage. Yet these barriers are falling rapidly. Bandwidth and disk space are

176 THE FUTURE OF RESOURCE SHARING

commodities, and even if demand is always slightly ahead of supply, the supply continues to grow. As for the ramping up of telecommunication speed, one does not have to be very old to remember 300 baud acoustical couplers.

Publishers are taking an initiative in a number of image delivery projects. The TULIP project, spearheaded by Elsevier in cooperation with a number of other science, technological, and medical publishers has been around for several years. Springer's Red Sage project, and AT&T's RightPages are other promising developments. Still in the planning stages, the Oasis project is a proposed cooperative project of a group of (important) publishers in the U.K. who are investigating ways to offer article image files, and examining the commercial feasibility of this type of undertaking.

The attractive feature to the publisher of these types of products is that they maintain control of the images they own. Publishers can collect royalties directly from the user. Even though downstreaming of the image is still a possibility, because the publisher has a one-to-one relationship with the purchaser of the image files, the publisher is in a better position to monitor use and safeguard against misuse.

The downside of publisher-direct document delivery services, particularly in the image delivery arena, but also in the fax or paper delivery world, is that publishers are not usually in a position to support the level of computing necessary to link to networks and to develop and support a search interface. Publicly accessible, easy to use computer databases do not come cheaply. Ask any library. Some publishers are technologically advanced with resources enough to launch this kind of a service; many are not.

COOPERATIVE VENTURES

Cooperative ventures between libraries and publishers (such as TULIP and Red Sage), between publishers and document delivery vendors, and between vendors and libraries hold great promise. A pilot project of John Wiley & Sons and the UnCover Company is a model for publisher and document delivery vendor cooperation. In the future, this arrangement could easily provide answers to some of the problems noted above. Wiley and UnCover are jointly sponsoring a pilot project that uses the UnCover database as a locating tool for articles in Wiley periodicals.

When a user places an order for an article contained in a Wiley publication the order information is shipped over a high speed line to the Wiley offices in New York. The request is filled from Wiley's own database of article images. UnCover handles the collection of a service fee and the copyright payment.

An important part of the project is the supply to UnCover of Wiley table of contents information, called headers, in standard generalized mark-up language (SGML). The header information contains abstracts, not found on the table of contents of the print publication. The SGML format allows machine readable data to be loaded directly into the UnCover database, eliminating the need for keyboard entry from the issue itself.

The primary advantage to UnCover of this cooperation is reduced cost—both in the creation of the database and the fulfillment of the article request. Wiley benefits by the visibility in UnCover's database, searchable by a simple to use interface, and accessible on a network used by thousands of people worldwide. At the same time Wiley maintains control of its image database and receives royalties from its use.

Like publishers, vendors are projecting a new visibility among the end users, often in cooperative projects with the library. For example, the UnCover Company is cooperating on an unmediated document ordering project with Colorado State University (CSU) library. University students, faculty, and staff are able to order articles directly from UnCover from terminals in the library. The CSU library subsidizes the payment of all articles ordered from titles not held within the library's collection. UnCover assists in this project by insuring that the user is authorized by the library before allowing him to place an order, and by blocking ordering from CSU owned materials. Once the system, designed in partnership between librarians and UnCover, was implemented, unmediated searching and ordering by CSU patrons freed librarians to turn their attention to more complex service challenges.

WHERE DO WE GO FROM HERE?

The Internet is a good analogy for the future of document delivery suppliers. The Internet, which started with a limited number of users and resources, has quickly grown to serve millions of users and has more databases and resources than most people will ever be able to find and utilize. Almost as soon as the amount of available information became unmanageable, helpful programs and databases such as Archie, Hytelnet and Veronica were created to aid users in locating and utilizing available resources. The next step was the development of interfaces such as Gopher and Mosaic to help the average user navigate the Internet. User friendly graphical interfaces to these information sources transform database searching almost to the level of entertainment, and certainly remove the threat for even the most serious computer-phobes. Document delivery vendors are now positioned to make the delivery process easier for librarian and end user alike.

Earlier in this article it was suggested that the document delivery vendor may in the future become simply an unnecessary intermediary. Publishers might just as easily deliver their products directly to libraries via electronic networks. Or, directly to the reader, making the library yet another unneeded intermediary. Just as the Internet grows, the publishing world continues to grow at an incredible pace. Already, libraries seldom deal with publishers directly. The process of going directly to the publisher has become as overwhelming as navigating the Internet without the tools described above. For printed items, libraries usually develop a relationship with the publisher directly only if their book vendor does not handle the publisher or if the items from that publisher are of special interest. Publishers, too, would be hard pressed to establish and maintain contacts with every library and individual who wants their materials.

Publishers generally are not prepared to recreate the kinds of computer networks, database designs, and search engines currently offered by established online public access catalog providers like OCLC, CARL, and increasingly, the integrated online library management systems. Even if they were, would the end user, be it the library or the individual reader, be willing to deal with potentially hundreds of different publisher front-ends to access needed materials? The document delivery vendor provides a clearinghouse function for the user and a service bureau function for the publisher. No publisher would cut out an established marketer, with a ready-made clientele, eager to sell a product.

We must also pose the question: will the information consumer be willing to forego the navigational assistance provided by both the library and the document delivery vendor through the ever increasing mass of information offered along the highway? Isn't the vendor, like the library, a valuable intermediary, with skills in networking, interface writing, and understanding user needs.

If a product is to be accepted by the librarian and end-user, it must not only be simple to use, but there must also be real people behind it to aid users in utilizing the product. Businesses that are successful not only provide a product, but also provide a human interface for those purchasing the product. In the retail arena, Walmart can be used as an example. This very successful store has many "human-touches" such as the door greeter found at every Walmart store, as well as a very liberal return policy. Walmart provides a good example of mixing human interaction with a wide variety of products sold at competitive prices. The document supplier can provide the human interface among client, document, publisher, and computer.

Computers are required to provide the ordering and delivery methods required for a 24-48 hour turnaround time. However, not all computer users are alike. The UnCover service has users from throughout the world and the service was created to allow anyone accessing the database to order articles for delivery. Although UnCover has clients who have never contacted the company, Uncover staff has responded to a number of clients personally, some with special needs regarding access or payment.

The document delivery supplier has the role of simplifying the identification and ordering processes. The document supplier can simplify the process of identifying for information sources for end users by contracting with a large number of publishers and offering their information in a single location. The document supplier can simplify the ordering process by offering end users a choice of convenient payment methods and by relieving the publisher of the burden of billing and collecting from a large number of individual users.

Document delivery suppliers can also enhance these processes by providing usage statistics and detailed financial reports to both publisher and end user. The end user can also benefit from a document supplier's ability to manage copyright. Smaller publishers can use document suppliers as a service bureau, which will reduce the num-

180   THE FUTURE OF RESOURCE SHARING

ber of staff and other resources required to get information out to a large audience. For larger publishers, document delivery suppliers will act as marketing partners, offering exposure and an additional method for the clients to access the data.

We must be sure that in the information democracy we don't lose the valuable services provided by database and document delivery vendors–those of designing systems, followed by archiving and filtering information. Gophers are a marvelous invention, but they offer crude search engines and are limited in their ability to present material in a usable fashion. The role of the successful vendor, like the skilled librarian, is to organize the content for our markets, and to optimize the use of the technology available.

Pamela Bluh, writing in the February 1993 issue of *Wilson Library Bulletin*, cautions against the de-humanizing effect of the unmediated environment toward which we are moving and urges librarians to take a proactive stance to promote new services and educate users about the value of the resources. She has this to say about document delivery:

> The successful document delivery service will be multifaceted. It will anticipate users' needs as well as offer them access to material in a timely fashion, and it will be fully integrated with other library operations yet flexible and procedurally straightforward to use while remaining cost-effective.[5]

The future belongs to document delivery that is "multifaceted, timely, and cost-effective," or in other words, better, faster, cheaper. Yet it needs to have a human touch as well. For the vendor this means a human voice at the end of a telephone line, a way to locate materials that does not require knowledge of jargon or arcane search strategies, and delivery mechanisms that are widely available and make the optimum use of popular technology.

NOTES

1. Kurosman, Kathleen, and Barbara Ammerman Durniak, "Document Delivery: A comparison of commercial document suppliers and interlibrary loan services," in *College & Research Libraries* (March 1994), pp. 129-138.

2. Roche, Marilyn M., *ARL/RLG Interlibrary Loan Cost Study*, Association of Research Libraries, 1993.

3. Okerson, Ann "With Feathers: Effects of copyright and ownership on scholarly publishing." *College & Research Libraries*, v.52, no.5, Sept. 1991, pp. 425-438.

4. "CCC to Collectively License Digital Uses of Full Text," *Online Newsletter*, v.15, no. 4, April 1994, p.1.

5. Bluh, Pamela, "Document Delivery 2000: Will It Change the Nature of Librarianship?" *Wilson Library Bulletin*, v.67, no.6, Feb. 1993, pp. 49-51.

Staff and Training Issues: Optimizing the Potential of Library Partnerships

Jack Siggins

GROWTH OF INTEREST IN RESOURCE SHARING

Increasingly libraries are coming under pressure to accommodate users who wish to have greater and faster access to information sources. The world of research seems to be drawing closer to the ultimate goal of having instant access to all information at all times. Ten years ago faculty and students might have expressed their expectation of the library simply as: "All I ask is that, when I go to the library to look for something, the book I want will be on the shelf." Today they are more likely to express it as: "All I ask is that you provide me quick access to everything out there I might want." Whereas ten years ago the primary emphasis was still on finding and obtaining *what* was needed from the library, now the issue of *when* an article or book can be obtained is becoming as important as gaining access to it.

Mediation–in which librarians assist users to get to information sources–is still the dominant method of library service to users today. Disintermediation–in which users gain access to an informa-

---

Jack Siggins is University Librarian at George Washington University in Washington, DC.

[Haworth co-indexing entry note]: "Staff and Training Issues: Optimizing the Potential of Library Partnerships." Siggins, Jack. Co-published simultaneously in *Journal of Library Administration* (The Haworth Press, Inc.) Vol. 21, No. 1/2, 1995, pp. 183-191; and *The Future of Resource Sharing* (ed: Shirley K. Baker, and Mary E. Jackson) The Haworth Press, Inc., 1995, pp. 183-191. Multiple copies of this article/chapter may be purchased from The Haworth Document Delivery Center [1-800-342-9678; 9:00 a.m. - 5:00 p.m. (EST)].

© 1995 by The Haworth Press, Inc. All rights reserved.   *183*

184   THE FUTURE OF RESOURCE SHARING

tion system without assistance or mediation from a librarian–increasingly, however, is the standard by which the effectiveness of libraries will be assessed. While mediation is still a fact of daily life within libraries, disintermediation is becoming the goal. Consequently, librarians today are faced with both a search problem (identifying the location of information) and an inventory control problem (organizing, storing and accessing information).

Librarians are just beginning to build the infrastructure for electronic information service delivery at the same time they are faced with stagnant or decreasing budgetary support. They are still novices at providing access outside their own library, especially electronic access. The budgeting process at universities doesn't yet adequately accommodate access service planning. Today library staff must be comfortable with change and technology, and be able to handle ambiguity.

Because of the pressures from declining resources on the one hand and growing demand for services on the other, one of the solutions many library directors are turning to is resource sharing. Reorganization (or re-engineering) of library work activities is another response, as indicated by organizational restructuring efforts recently initiated in the libraries of institutions such as Boston College, the University of Arizona, the University of Louisville, and the University of Missouri, just to mention a few. As cooperative resource sharing agreements among libraries become more common, greater numbers of staff will be faced with major changes in their jobs. They will be required to alter their work activities and reassess their places in the library organization.

IMPORTANCE OF PREPARING STAFF
FOR RESOURCE SHARING

In any effort involving a major shift of staff assignments or change in focus, consideration of the impact on staff is critical to success. Because they are on the front line of providing service and are consequently closer to users, staff know best what work needs to be done and how best to accomplish it. They know better than anyone what users need in the way of library services. Staff, especially those in reference and collection development, are usually the first among all library staff to recognize how service demands are evolving. They have first hand information which administrators often do not have and cannot easily acquire in today's work places. The technical infrastructure of most libraries is more highly developed than human systems. It is more likely that a librarian will know how to operate a sophisticated computer than to negotiate an agreement for resource sharing. Both technical expertise and negotiation skills are major requirements in modern libraries.

Three kinds of training need to be considered with regard to resource sharing: (1) for library selectors who are required to be experts in resource sharing processes and practices; (2) for staff directly involved in developing resource sharing agreements; and (3) for staff who must adjust to stress brought on by change and reorganization. Library directors who fail to recognize and provide for these three training needs run the risk of impeding the ability of their libraries to respond to changes in service demands.

WHAT RESOURCE SHARING REQUIRES OF STAFF

Consider this increasingly common scenario: You are a bibliographer or selector who has been given the assignment by your director to develop for your library a cooperative resource sharing agreement with several other libraries. It is expected that such an agreement will greatly benefit your library and its users by making available more efficiently a wide range of resources. It is expected that some relief from budgetary pressures will also be a result. In other words, it is a matter of great importance to your library. Then you sit down with representatives from the other participating libraries, some of whom you know and some whom you do not. What do you do if: (1) you find conflict among the representatives; (2) you can't reach agreement; and/or (3) you find yourself getting bogged down or side-tracked by endless discussion and wrangling?

The solution lies primarily in training in techniques of interactive group skills, reaching consensus, and leadership development. Despite this fact, however, in all the library literature written over the last several years dealing with resource sharing and cooperative collection development, rarely is there mention of the role of staff in these fundamental processes. There is even less discussion of the

186 THE FUTURE OF RESOURCE SHARING

need for staff training for resource sharing. The emphasis instead has been on the technicalities of what an agreement should include. When a library undertakes a serious effort at resource sharing, whether within the context of a formal consortial organization or simply with one or more libraries with similar interests, staff are affected significantly. An alert library administrator will be aware of this fact, analyze how that impact will manifest itself and then take steps to meet that need.

Resource sharing places stress on staff in three areas: education, attitude and skills.

Education. Staff must acquire an understanding of the processes of resource sharing. They must have a thorough understanding of what resource sharing entails and why it is important to the library both today and in the future. The degree to which they are able to develop a certain sophistication and breadth of knowledge will depend upon their level of responsibility and involvement in resource sharing functions.

Attitude. Because resource sharing involves a shift in emphasis from acquisition and ownership of materials by the home institution to shared acquisition and remote access, staff must adjust their service philosophy. They must adopt a new way of approaching the task of providing service and meeting user needs.

Skills. Even more than education and attitude, skills of the staff are affected by resource sharing. Some new skills must be acquired, while at the same time greater emphasis is placed on some older skills, such as neutral questioning in which users are queried more closely about the urgency and time limitations of their requests. The addition of new, time consuming tasks arising from the development and implementation of resource sharing agreements enhances the need for effective time management. The shift in the focus of collection development to a combination of local purchase, shared collecting responsibilities, and remote accessing requires adjustments in planning and priorities. Advanced interpersonal skills must also be present in staff in order to conduct more effectively the dual responsibilities of reaching agreements and explaining them to users. Among these required interpersonal skills are communication, negotiation, conflict resolution, managing change, self-leadership, and the ability to interpret goals to staff, users, and administrators. Conceptual skills are also necessary. Staff will need to be more effective in such tasks as problem-solving, decision-making, process improvement, critical thinking, and creativity.

As resource sharing is introduced to a greater extent in libraries, several changes will begin to develop in the way in which staff perform their assignments, as well as in the assignments themselves. To the extent they are made aware in advance of these changes and have been prepared for them through training, staff will be able to adapt to the new environment with greater or lesser ease.

One important impact will be the working relationship between professional and support staff. The distinction made today between tasks performed by professional librarians and those by support staff will become even more blurred than they already are. Support staff will take over some tasks currently the responsibility of professional librarians who in turn will assume new assignments and activities. Instead of focusing on differences and on a code of strict adherence to assigned levels of tasks, emphasis will be placed on partnerships between professionals and support staff as they respond to the need for cooperation in accomplishing unit and departmental assignments. Resource sharing is one of many areas of library operations in which teams of staff will be developed and will be expected to work together. Each member of a team will be expected to contribute to a group effort. This new relationship will require staff to adopt a different, more collaborative approach to decision-making and division of assignments. It can also benefit greatly from training.

Staff will also be expected to be aware of new job demands being placed upon them as soon as they begin to appear. Library jobs are evolutionary, changing steadily due to pressures from advances in technology, automation, and other influences. Administrators will have to be alert to the need for re-training of staff resulting from this gradual change. They will also need to ask questions about work assignments, such as: "Is the work properly designed?" and "Is the job described accurately and classified correctly?" As resource sharing becomes more of a major factor of library work, these issues will need to be addressed regularly.

Change produces stress which can be either a negative force, if it

188 THE FUTURE OF RESOURCE SHARING

decreases efficiency and job satisfaction among staff. or a positive element, if it leads to creativity and innovation. The difference in response to change on the part of staff can be greatly influenced by preparing staff for change in advance through training.

PREPARING AND TRAINING STAFF FOR RESOURCE SHARING

The most effective resource sharing staff will be those who accept change as part of organizational life and who embrace continuous improvement as a necessary and desirable element of their job. The learning individual, like the learning organization, can be a self-perpetuating, positive influence on the quality of job performance. To encourage a positive response, staff should also have variety in work assignments and the feeling that they are part of an important, ongoing process, not just slotted into narrow job descriptions.

The task of preparing and training staff begins with the recognition that they are being asked to apply new learning to their already existing base of knowledge. Staff bring to the training process a certain level of insight and understanding about library activities. As a result, some "unlearning" may be necessary along with the learning; that is, while some experience and practices will be directly applicable and beneficial to the effort to develop resource sharing skills, others may be a hinderance. An example of contributing experience would be the ability to identify user needs, while a hindering practice might be the tendency to work alone with little or no reliance on others for input into the collection development decision-making process.

It is important to understand that much of the learning process in resource sharing will occur on the job; that is, while it is being conducted. Although the principles and policies may be easily explained in training, most knowledge will eventually be gained by actually doing the work.

Of equal importance is the fact that library administrators should address certain broad issues before providing the actual training. Staff need to be prepared to accept change. Library vision and values need to be clarified. New performance expectations and work environments should be identified. The role of technology as an important tool of the library should be well understood. New paradigms of library work and working relationships should be described. Staff should be guided in techniques of learning how to learn. Continuous learning as a key element in the library's culture generally and in resource sharing specifically should be inculcated in staff. Finally, administrators should acknowledge that these efforts will require both organizational support and staff time for learning.

METHODS AND APPROACHES

A combination of both group and individual training methods should be used to prepare staff for resource sharing. Each person has a predominant learning profile; that is, each of us has a preferred strategy or style for learning. A person's learning style determines his or her ability to absorb new projects, enhance capabilities, contribute to a team's results, and get in synch with the other staff members. Since each staff member will bring to the training process certain learning skills and experiences, an assessment should first be made of each individual's learning style preferences. A training program then can be developed incorporating these various preferences. In a team setting, developing a good mix of learning styles can be critical to the team's success. Diagnostic instruments, such as the Learning Style Inventory or the Learning Style Diagnostic Questionnaire, may be used to discover the learning style of an individual or the profile of a team.[1]

In some instances, one-on-one training may be the most effective method, allowing a more experienced person to serve as mentor for a less experienced staff member. Another technique is cooperative or collaborative learning, in which individuals or groups share what they know of a certain process or subject with another individual or group.

The most common practice for training staff in resource sharing is the use of workshops and classrooms conducted by experts in the subject. These include both on-site and off-site events. They can be conducted by knowledgeable in-house staff, if they are available, or by outsiders who bring with them experience in developing and implementing resource sharing programs elsewhere. Whoever is given this responsibility, however, must have proven skills in staff training and development, as well as in resource sharing.

MODEL FOR TRAINING WORKSHOP IN RESOURCE SHARING

The following are topics which should be included in any workshop or training program in resource sharing:

- Key assumptions about resource sharing and cooperative collection development
- Benefits and drawbacks of resource sharing
- Types of resource sharing projects
- Planning process, including
  - environmental scan
  - problems/needs/risks
  - idea generation
- Strategies for responding to library budget issues
- Developing project ideas
- Developing cooperative agreements
- Assessing organizational impact
- Measuring success
- Interpreting resource sharing to key stakeholders

CONCLUSIONS

Resource sharing is a partial solution to library budget problems whose time has definitely arrived. It clearly will be a major part of library strategies and planning for the future. It is also an exciting opportunity for improving library services.

At the same time, resource sharing presents both opportunities and challenges for library staff and administrators. Library staff need to prepare themselves for the changes arising from resource sharing by adopting a collaborative process in which they learn from each other. This process should be one of discovery in which improved ways of meeting user needs are constantly created.

AUTHOR NOTE

The author wishes to acknowledge the contributions to the ideas presented in this paper made by two colleagues, Maureen Sullivan and George Soete, with whom he has worked in developing and conducting workshops on resource sharing and other library staff training topics.

NOTE

1. Peter M. Senge et al., *The Fifth Discipline Fieldbook: Strategies and Tools for Building a Learning Organization* (New York: Doubleday, 1994): 421. See also: David A. Kolb, *Experiential Learning (Englewood Cliffs, N.J.: Prentice-Hall, 1994)*.

The Future of Resource Sharing: The Role of the Association of Research Libraries

Mary E. Jackson

INTRODUCTION

Academic and research libraries are growing more interdependent for access to scholarly and research materials. Historically, large academic and research libraries have been the source for materials needed by other libraries. Increasingly, these libraries are being asked to build local collections but simultaneously provide access to materials not purchased locally.

The Association of Research Libraries (ARL) is an organization representing the interests of 119 libraries that serve major North American institutions. In 1991, ARL's Committee on Access to Research Resources prepared a white paper, "Evolution of Electronic Resource Sharing,"[1] that summarized the array of issues associated with providing access in a networked environment. Discussion of the white paper at the October 1991 Membership Meeting identified two priority activities for the Access Committee:

1. Reconceptualize interlibrary loan and document delivery, employing technology to make it less labor-intensive and

---

Mary E. Jackson is Access and Delivery Services Consultant for The Association of Research Libraries in Washington, DC.

[Haworth co-indexing entry note]: "The Future of Resource Sharing: The Role of the Association of Research Libraries." Jackson, Mary E. Co-published simultaneously in *Journal of Library Administration* (The Haworth Press, Inc.) Vol. 21, No. 1/2, 1995, pp. 193-202; and *The Future of Resource Sharing* (ed: Shirley K. Baker, and Mary E. Jackson) The Haworth Press, Inc., 1995, pp. 193-202. Multiple copies of this article/chapter may be purchased from The Haworth Document Delivery Center [1-800-342-9678; 9:00 a.m. - 5:00 p.m. (EST)].

© 1995 by The Haworth Press, Inc. All rights reserved.

identify cost models for alternative configurations and delivery mechanisms, and

2. Reconceptualize the values and principles that provide the underpinnings of electronic resource sharing.

Building on the Access Committee's work, Shirley K. Baker, Dean of University Libraries at Washington University in Saint Louis, and this author collaborated on a second white paper for the Access Committee. This paper, "Maximizing Access, Minimizing Cost: A First Step Toward the Information Access Future,"[2] reviewed the current interlibrary loan environment, critiqued ILL processes, and described an ideal interlibrary loan and document delivery system. Additional sections included descriptions of an ideal ILL management system and an ideal financial tracking system. The paper also listed eleven activities and actions the authors identified as necessary to move toward the ideal.

The Baker/Jackson white paper was shared widely with the library community through a series of presentations at local, state, and national library association meetings. The paper was also presented to library utilities, local system providers, document delivery suppliers, and other vendors that provide services and products for the ILL/DD market.

Emerging from the discussions of the Baker/Jackson white paper was the identification of a series of desirable technical improvements and system design enhancements. Discussions and conversations with representatives of the vendor community substantiated the belief that pieces of the solution already exist, but that a comprehensive and integrated approach was required. These discussions also confirmed that the commercial sector, rather than the ARL as an association, was the appropriate source for the technical and systems enhancements. ARL was prepared to play a major role in supporting a visible focus on these technical developments and systems enhancements.

In the summer of 1994, ARL hosted an open meeting to which over fifty organizations, individuals, and companies were invited. This meeting was held during the American Library Association's Annual Conference. The Vendor Forum formalized the process by which ARL would encourage and pursue required technical developments and system enhancements. Two groups were established as a result of the Vendor Forum. The first, the Developers/Implementors Group (DIG), was composed of organizations in a position to commit to develop one or more components of the Project. The second, the Informational Group, was established for those organizations not in a position to commit to develop a product or service, but interested in monitoring the progress of the Project.

Three Working Groups have been established within the Developers/Implementors Group, each focusing on one of the three Project's objectives. The Management System Working Group is concentrating on the development of comprehensive management software. The Financial/Accounting Working Group is examining ways to improve the process of paying for ILL transactions. The Standards Working Group is identifying potential areas for standards development and drafting standards that will permit the linkage of disparate components of the total ILL process.

MANAGEMENT SYSTEM WORKING GROUP

The internal management of interlibrary loan operations has not been completely automated. Library-to-library requesting has been successfully automated with the ILL systems developed by OCLC, RLG, WLN, and the National Library of Medicine. ILL requests are now rarely mailed to potential suppliers; most of this library-to-library communication has been automated. Many ILL departments also use their local circulation systems for tracking loaned materials; some also charge materials borrowed for their local patrons on their circulation systems.

Missing from the ILL department is comprehensive software that would automate internal processing. Several ILL software programs have been developed, but none is comprehensive. The need to reduce the labor-intensive, and costly, nature of ILL processing is critical. Since 77% of the unit cost of an ILL transaction is staffing,[3] any software that would reduce or eliminate filing, data gathering, statistics generation, and/or report writing offers the potential to reduce the unit cost of an ILL transaction.

The Management System Working Group reached consensus on the general components of a comprehensive ILL/DD management

THE FUTURE OF RESOURCE SHARING

system and developed a document that describes the system in some detail.[4]

FINANCIAL/ACCOUNTING WORKING GROUP

It is becoming more common for libraries to charge for supplying loans or providing photocopies. Most of these charges are transaction-based, although some libraries have established no-charge reciprocal agreements in order to avoid problems associated with invoicing. Library suppliers have a variety of methods of charging: invoices sent with the material, sent separately, or detailed on statements. Payment methods are equally varied: prepayment may be required, coupons may be required, deposit accounts encouraged, or payment may be required in the form of an institutional check.

Directors of ARL institutions held a spirited debate on the pros and cons of charging for interlibrary loan transactions. Because of deeply-held differences in opinion, ARL is neutral on the position of ILL charging, but does support efforts to reduce the labor-intensive nature of invoicing for those libraries that charge.

Members of the Developers/Implementors Group defined four alternative approaches to handle ILL charging. Two of the alternatives emerged as ones with the greatest potential to achieve significant short-term benefits. The first is the incorporation of an ILL billing system into one or more of the national ILL messaging systems. The second is the incorporation of a billing module into the comprehensive management software.

As with the management system, the Financial/Accounting Working Group reached consensus on the general components of an ILL/DD financial system and developed a detailed description of such a system.[5]

STANDARDS WORKING GROUP

Implicit in any description of an ideal ILL environment is the ability to move citations and requests electronically between and among citation databases, online catalogs, local ILL management software, and national ILL messaging systems. U.S. and international standards currently support portions of that communication, but again standards do not exist to support complete electronic passing of data.

The international ILL standards, *Interlibrary Loan Application Service Definition* and *Interlibrary Loan Application Protocol Specification* most effectively support the library-to-library communication. The NISO standards for Information Retrieval[6] and Interlibrary Loan Data Elements[7] support searching and the proper terms used in ILL requests respectively. Representatives from both standards organizations are actively participating in the Standards Working Group.

The Standards Working Group examined the range of possible standards needed to support complete electronic transfer. The Group's initial efforts have focused on the development of a standard for the patron request portion of the process. Standards for ILL policy directories and statistics are also being drafted.

THE NAILDD PROJECT IMPERATIVE

The Project's three technical objectives are clearly short-term steps needed before more substantive changes to the ILL process can be achieved. The focus of the Project has centered on these short-term needs for ILL departments. Members of the ARL Access Committee articulated the need for short-term, and reachable, objectives because there is general agreement that interlibrary loan departments will become key as libraries embrace the access service model. The process of sharing materials will continue, but weaknesses in the current ILL process must be eliminated if libraries, and our library users, are to consider the access service model successful. Many ILL departments are on the verge of collapse as a result of inefficient procedures, shortages of equipment and technology, outdated policies, and lack of vision of a new service model by some library staff.

BEYOND TECHNICAL ENHANCEMENTS

The profession's desire to improve interlibrary loan and document delivery by reducing turnaround time, improving fill rate, and

198   *THE FUTURE OF RESOURCE SHARING*

increasing user satisfaction was not going to be achieved by technical and system improvements alone. The need to review and improve local policies and procedures concurrent with the technical developments became apparent as a result of a series of informal discussions with members of the DIG, ILL managers, and library administrators. Technical improvements alone will not solve all the problems associated with the current ILL process. Borrowing and lending policies reflect a variety of local and historical factors. Some suggest that many of the current ILL policies and procedures were developed more to ease the workload of ILL staff than to provide timely service to ILL patrons.

In the Spring of 1994, the NAILDD Project sponsored a retreat for members of the Access Committee. The retreat was designed as an institutional effort requiring the participation of the library director, the head of public services, the head of access services, and the ILL manager. Position titles varied within an institution, but teams represented the local reporting structure from the ILL manager to library director. The retreat was designed and facilitated by Susan Jurow and Maureen Sullivan of ARL's Office of Management Services.

Participants in the initial retreat were led through a series of small-group activities developed to help the participants construct an "ideal" service model and identify those steps needed to move the local institution toward that ideal. Participants described the ideal service model as one in which users would order and receive materials primarily in an unmediated manner, but a model that was supported by appropriate library-mediated services and strong library collections.

Evaluations from the retreat confirmed the need for team-based examination of ILL service models. The retreat was renamed the Redesigning ILL/DD Institute and was held two additional times in 1994, with plans to hold additional Institutes in 1995.

THE VISION: UNMEDIATED SERVICE

Some have characterized the future of interlibrary loan as one in which library users will only use ILL departments when they are unable to locate materials themselves. Technology, policies, and services will all be designed to minimize staff involvement in the ILL process. ILL staff will be needed to handle very specialized or unique requests.

It is clear that libraries will move toward this future vision at different rates. However, as libraries embrace this unmediated service model, new definitions of "success" must be developed. Currently, successful ILL departments are generally measured on the volume of borrowing and lending requests processed. A second measure of ILL is that of cost, as witnessed by the publication of the *ARL/RLG Interlibrary Loan Cost Study*.[8] The new service model cannot be measured by volume and cost alone.

The success of the new service model will include additional performance measures. These measures will count not only volume of activity and cost, but will include turnaround time, fill rate, and user satisfaction. Currently, many libraries track turnaround time and fill rates, but national level data are not collected. User satisfaction is often measured by the number of complimentary letters received by ILL departments or by the number of acknowledgements, especially in dissertations and theses. ARL and other organizations will play a leading role in defining the performance measures to measure "success" of this new service model.

UNRESOLVED ISSUES

To suggest that the future service model can be implemented simply and easily is grossly misleading. A number of other factors will influence the way in which this service model is ultimately defined. These factors include the digitization of existing library materials, increased electronic publishing initiatives, development of electronic delivery technologies, concerns about copyright compliance, increased use of and reliance on libraries and suppliers internationally, access to non-library document delivery suppliers, and national and international standards.

The digitization of library collections and the rate with which publishers will make materials available in electronic format each will affect the way in which users will gain access to published material. Optimists predict that the combination of library-based digitization projects of older and/or non-copyrighted materials with

THE FUTURE OF RESOURCE SHARING

widespread electronic publication will eliminate the need for ILL departments. Pessimists argue that digitization and electronic publishing initiatives will only marginally change the way in which library users gain access to needed materials.

Improvements to existing electronic delivery technologies such as the Research Libraries Group's Ariel and the development of new technologies such as MIME will improve the delivery of materials to libraries. In the new service model, these technologies will deliver materials directly to individuals as appropriate. Combined with access to databases and online ordering capabilities, electronic delivery technologies offer the promise of desktop delivery to support unmediated service.

Knowledge of and compliance with the copyright laws and related guidelines will remain critical in the new service model. One of the outgrowth's of the Clinton/Gore focus on the development of the National Information Infrastructure (NII) has been the appointment of the Working Group on Intellectual Property Rights, one of the working groups of the Information Infrastructure Task Force. The preliminary draft report of the Working Group on Intellectual Property Rights, *Intellectual Property and the National Information Infrastructure*,[9] or the "green paper," examines the intellectual property implications of the NII. The NII will certainly be used for interlibrary loan and document delivery activities. A future service model may be shaped by recommendations and outcomes of the NII Working Groups.

Electronic requesting and delivery technologies are shrinking the world of potential suppliers. In this new service model, it is easy to imagine the importance of libraries worldwide in providing timely delivery of needed material. As libraries outside North America assume more active roles in the distributed "national" collection projects, these libraries may increase the success of traditional ILL services.

In a similar manner, document suppliers will also play a more central role in this new service model. Currently, many ILL departments use document suppliers as a supplement to their primary library sources.[10] As existing document suppliers expand their coverage and as new document suppliers are introduced, library users may prefer to choose document suppliers over interlibrary loan departments because of ease of use or timely delivery. In this new service model, document suppliers may play a more central role.

As mentioned earlier, standards will continue to assume a core role in the new service model. New national and international standards need to be written to improve segments of this new service model. It is not an understatement to suggest that the success of the new ILL/DD service model will be based on national and international standards.

CONCLUSION

The future of resource sharing, of interlibrary loan, of document delivery, of "electronic article sharing" is promising. Libraries are reexamining the ways in which they provide access to scholarly materials. Ownership will continue to be the preferred method of providing access, but remotely held materials will increase in importance.

The Association of Research Libraries will continue to play a leadership role in promoting effective ILL/DD service models, providing training opportunities, and encouraging the commercial sector to develop new services and technologies that will ensure the success of resource sharing for North American libraries.

Resource sharing has been broadly defined to include ILL, document delivery, onsite access, and local ownership. The future of resource sharing will succeed when physical resources, policies, personnel, and practices are organized to provide timely information delivery to library users.

NOTES

1. "Evolution of Electronic Resource Sharing: A White Paper Prepared by the ARL Committee on Access to Information Resources for the October 1991 Membership Meeting."

2. *Maximizing Access, Minimizing Costs: A First Step Toward the Information Access Future,* prepared by Shirley K. Baker and Mary E. Jackson for the ARL Committee on Access to Information Resources. November 1992, Revised February 1993.

3. Marilyn M. Roche, *ARL/RLG Interlibrary Loan Cost Study.* Washington, D.C. Association of Research Libraries, June 1993, p. 12.

4. "North American Interlibrary Loan/Document Delivery (NAILDD) Project ILL/DD Management System: Summary Description." Prepared by Mary E. Jackson. January, 1994.

5. "North American Interlibrary Loan/Document Delivery (NAILDD) Project ILL/DD Financial System: Summary Description." Prepared by Mary E. Jackson. January, 1994.

6. *Information Retrieval Application Service Definition and Protocol Specification for Open Systems Interconnection*. ANSI/NISO Z39.50-1992. New Brunswick, NJ, Transaction Publishers, 1993.

7. *Interlibrary Loan Data Elements*. ANSI/NISO Z39.63-1989. New Brunswick, NJ, Transaction Publishers, 1990.

8. Marilyn M. Roche, *ARL/RLG Interlibrary Loan Cost Study*, Washington. DC, Association of Research Libraries, June 1993.

9. *Intellectual Property and the National Information Infrastructure; A Preliminary Draft of the Report of the Working Group on Intellectual Property Rights*, Information Infrastructure Task Force, July, 1994.

10. *Uses of Document Delivery Services. A SPEC Kit compiled by Mary E. Jackson and Karen Croneis*. SPEC Kit #204, Washington, DC, Association of Research Libraries, November, 1994.

Index

Note: Page numbers followed by f indicate figures.

Academic disciplines, redefinition
    of, 14
Academic libraries, scholarly
    journals in, 55
Access
  defined, 121
  to networked holdings, 124-127
Accessibility
  beyond, 46-47
  bibliographic, age of, 39-40
  costs of, 40-43,41f-43f
  of information, future of, 45-46
  vs. ownership, 44-45
Archives, described, 18
Aries, P., 14
ARL North American Interlibrary
    Loan/Document Delivery
    Project, 36
ARL/RLG ILL Cost Study, 128, 199
Association of Research Libraries
    (ARL)
  beyond technical enhancements,
    197-198
  described, 193
  Financial/Accounting Working
    Group in, 196
  Management System Working
    Group in, 195-196
  monography and serial costs in,
    42f
  NAILDD initiative of, 145-167.
    See also North American
    Interlibrary Loan and
    Document Delivery
    (NAILDD) initiative
  NAILDD Project Imperative in,
    197

resources per student, 43f
role in resource sharing, 193-201
spendings of, 7
Standards Working Group in,
    196-197
statement on copyright law, 50
unresolved issues related to,
    199-201
vision of, 198-199
Atkinson, H., 61
Attitude, for resource sharing, 186

Baker, S. K., 194
Barter, as mechanism for resource
    sharing, 79
Basic service, of document delivery
    services, 134
Bernal, J. D., 61
Bibliographic accessibility, age of,
    39-40
Bloch, M., 14
Bluh, P., 180
Boorstin, D., 13
Braudel, F., 14
Buck, P., 10
Burke, P., 13
Buyers' cooperative, 93-96,95f

Carnegie Mellon University libraries,
    Mercury project at, 125
Cataloging, copy, 40
Center for Research Libraries (CRL),
    32
CIC Virtual Electronic Library, 72

© 1995 by The Haworth Press, Inc. All rights reserved.

204 THE FUTURE OF RESOURCE SHARING

Coalition for Networked Information
(CNI), 32
Collaborative collection
development, integrated
regional model for, 20-22
Collection(s)
building of, 122-124
cancellations and decreased
purchasing power effects
on, 122
guidelines for, 122-123
implications of, 138-139
integrated regional model for,
20-22
lobbying for, 123
resource sharing in, 6-9
defined, 121
organization of, by electronic
information technologies,
68-70
Colorado State University (CSU),
library, 177
Columbia University Law Library,
Project Janus at, 125-126
Commission on New Technological
Uses of Copyrighted Works
(CONTU), guidelines of,
51
Committee on Institutional
Cooperation (CIC)
Libraries, 72
Communication
cost of, vs. storage costs, 86-88
electronic, fascination with, 15
Computing, distributed, in public
university library resource
sharing, 35-36
Consortia, in public university
library resource sharing, 32
redefined, 35
Continual quality improvement
(CQI), 138
Coolidge, A. C., 10, 15
Copy cataloging, 40

Copyright
prevailing interpretation of, 57
purpose of, 49-52
Copyright Clearance Center (CCC),
175
Copyright issues, in digital library
sharing, 8-9
Core services, defined, 33-34
Cost issues. *See* Financial
considerations
Current Contents on Diskette
(CCOD), 140

Data communication, cost of, vs.
storage costs, 86-88
De Gennaro, R., 6-7
Deluxe service, of document delivery
services, 135
Demand, vs. funding, 30-31
Digital information, described, 15
Disintermediation, 98-99
Distributed computing, in public
university library resource
sharing, 35-36
DOCLINE, 123
Document delivery
Academic library's perspective
on, 133-142
basic service, 134
better, faster, and cheaper,
171-172
charging for, 135
collection development policy
related to, 138-139
cooperative ventures of, 176-177
cost-benefit relationship in,
172-174
costs of, 44, 136-137
defined, 134
deluxe service, 135
demand for, 133
future directions in, 140-142
vendor's perspective on,
169-181
ideal system, 140-141

Index

image, 174-176
networks in, 172-174
policies for, 134-136
premium service, 134-135
revolutionizing, 46-47
suppliers of, selection and
evaluation of, 137-138
types of, 134
uses of
innovative, 139-140
value-added service, 135
Document type definitions (DTDs),
174-175
Dominguez, P., 73-74
Durniak, B. A., 171

Education, for resource sharing, 186
EJL. *See* Electronic Journal List
Electronic age, resource sharing in,
initiatives in, 70-72
Electronic communications,
fascination with, 15
Electronic data interchange (EDI),
159
Electronic delivery
of information, cost of, 85-86
of scholarly journals, 61-63
Electronic environment, resource
sharing in, initiatives in,
70-72
Electronic information technologies,
in organization of library
collections and services,
68-70
Electronic Journal List (EJL), 125
Electronic systems
cost of, 90-93,92f
and reader welfare, 105-107
Elsevier Science Publishers,
University LIcensing
Program with, 126
Engineering Information, Inc., 100
"Evolution of Electronic Resource
Sharing," 193
External supply cost per year, 89,90f

Financial/Accounting Working
Group, 196
Financial considerations
in document delivery service,
136-137
in NAILDD, 158-162
in OhioLINK experience, 112-114
in resource sharing, 77-107
Financial resources, for accessibility,
40-43,41f-43f
Flexibility, in acquisitions process,
139
Franklin, B., 79
Funding, vs. demand, 30-31

Gelman Library, 139-140
George Washington University (GW),
Gelman Library at, 139-140
Gourman, J., 87
Grant(s), as mechanism for resource
sharing, 81

Haldeman, H. R., 87
Harvard Library, structure of, 9-10
Hawkins, B., 7,20,32
History, subfields in, 12-13
Holdings information, 121-122
networked, access to, 124-127
Houghton, 61

ILL. *See* Interlibrary loan
Image delivery, 174-176
Industry, university partnerships
with, 29
Information
accessibility of, 45-46
prices for, role of, 77-78
storing of, cost of, 85
Information Exchange Group (IEG)
experiment, 61
Information technology
fascination with, 15

in public university library
resource sharing, 35-36
Innovative Interfaces, Inc., in
OhioLINK system, 110
Inquiry, changing methods of, 12-15
Integrated online library systems
(IOLS), 146
Integrated Regional Model, in
collection development,
20-22
*Intellectual Property and the
National Information
Infrastructure*, 200
Interlibrary loan (ILL)
history of, 1
NLM-automated, 123
role of, 127-130
of scholarly journals, 53
Interlibrary loan unit, future of, in
Ohio Library and
Information Network
(OhioLINK) experience,
116-118
Internet
described, 146
document delivery by, 170-180
Iowa State University, funding to, 28
ISI
CCOD at, 140
TGA at, 140

Jackson, M. E., 36,139
John Wiley & Sons, 176
Journal(s)
expensive, impact of, 59-61
scholarly. *See* Scholarly journals
subscription to, cost of, 59
Journal article
financial reward from, 56
funding of, 56
as information source, 58-59
number read, 58
prevailing interpretation of
copyright of, 57

production of
costliness of, 59
economic colonialism in, 57-58
publishers of, unfair subsidy for,
58
rudimentary access to, 57
time delay related to, 56-57
value of, 56

Kirby, W., 14
Kurosman, K., 171

Lanham, R., 15
Learning Style Diagnostic
Questionnaire, 189
Learning Style Inventory, 189
Lehman, B., 149
Library partnerships, staff and
training issues in, 183-190.
See also Resource sharing,
staff and training issues in
Library programs, factors affecting,
41f
Lobbying, in resource sharing, 123
Local electronic storage cost per
year, 91,92f
Local electronic storage cost with
acquisition, 95-96,97f

Management System Working
Group, 195-196
Market power, defined, 102
"Maximizing Access, Minimizing
Cost: A First Step Toward
the Information Access
Future," 194
Maxwell, R., 54
Mediation, defined, 183
MELVYL, 125
Monetary exchange, as mechanism
for resource sharing, 79-81
Morrill Act of 1862, 27

Index

NAILDD. *See* North American Interlibrary Loan and Document Delivery

NAILDD Project Imperative, 197

National Information Infrastructure (NII), Clinton/Gore focus on, 200

National Interlibrary Loan Code, revision of, 2

Network delivery cost per year, 91, 92f

Network with local license cost, 96, 97f

Network with shared license cost, 96, 97f

Nixon, R. M., 87

Nontraditional research materials, 17-18

North American digital library, building of, organizational challenges of, 70

North American Interlibrary Loan and Document Delivery (NAILDD) initiative
borrowing library perspective on, 162-164
driving forces of, 145-146
financial issues in, 158-162
implementation of, 145-167
models and architectures for, 150-158
responsibilities to patrons, 164-166
settlements for, 158-162

O'Connor, S. D., Justice, 49-50

Ohio Library and Information Network (OhioLINK)
background of, 110
membership in, 109-110
Request for Proposal for, 110

Ohio Library and Information Network (OhioLINK) experience
administrative perspective of, 111-114
cost issues in, 112-114
described, 110-111
future of, 116-118
operating perspective of, 114-118
ownership and independence in, 112
patron perspective of, 118-119
steps in, 110
training in, 115-116
workload and workflow in, 114-115

OhioLINK. *See* Ohio Library and Information Network

Okerson, A., 175

Online Computer Library Center, Inc. (OOLC), objectives of, 32

Open stack cost per year, 88, 90f

Osburn, C., 7-8, 11

Outreach, defined, 29

Ownership, vs. access, 44-45

Pergamon Press, scholarly journals and, 54

Pogo, 64

Premium service, of document delivery services, 134-135

Prices. *See also under* Financial considerations

Project Janus, at Columbia University Law Library, 125-126

Public universities, and the public good, 27-37. *See also under* University(ies), public

Publishers
image delivery by, 176
of journal articles, unfair subsidy for, 58
scholarly journal, 54

Publishing, scholarly
copyright and, 49-52
of journals, growth of, 53-55

208   *THE FUTURE OF RESOURCE SHARING*

Purdue University Libraries'
Technical Information
Service (TIS), 135

Red Sage project, 176
Religions, subfields in, 12
Remote storage cost per year, 89,90f
Research
changes in, new documentary
sources and, 13-14
implications of, 15-19
interdisciplinary, 16-17
multidisciplinary, 18
national system for, 22-24
resources for, national system of, 20
sources needed for, 17
support for, 18-19
in a transinstitutional
environment, 5-24
transinstitutionalization of, 16
Research libraries
access in, 121
commercial document delivery
and, 133-142
comprehensive, 9-12
cooperative arrangements among,
history of, 11
copying of material by, 50
funding to, decline in, 30-31
prosperity of, following World
War II, 10-11
research changes effect on, 16-19
resource sharing in, future of,
67-74. *See also* Resource
sharing, in research
libraries
scholarly journals in, importance
of, 52-53
self-sufficiency in, 9-12,12-15
shift of focus on, 8
Research materials, nontraditional,
17-18
Research university, resource sharing
in, 5-24

Resource(s), reallocation of, 34-35
Resource sharing
acquisitions process in, flexibility
within, 139
ARL's role in, 193-201
attitude in, 186
barter in, 79
challenges for, 19
cooperative buying in, 93-96, 95f
as cooperative collection
building, 6-9
costs in, 101-105
disintermediation in, 98-99
document requests in, origination
and initial routing of,
162-164
education for, 186
efficiency in, 6
electronic copyright issues in, 8-9
expectations for, 130-131
forces behind, 6
future of, 63-64
implications for, 31-36
grants in, 81
impact of holdings on, 121-131
access to holdings, 124-127
impediments to, 122-123
information delivery, 8
integrated approach to, 109-120.
See also Ohio Library and
Information Network
integration of disparate services
in, 99-101
interest in, growth of, 183-184
introduction to, 1-3
low cost, 85-88
mechanisms of, 78-84
monetary exchange in, 79-81
North American, models and
architectures for, 150-158
OhioLINK experience in,
109-120. *See also* Ohio
Library and Information
Network
and prices, 77-107

Index

public university library's
imperative, 27-37
reader welfare in, 105-107
in research libraries
changes in, 67-68
future of, 67-74
framework for moving
forward, 72-74
objectives of, 67
for self-sufficiency, 12-15
skills for, 186-187
staff and training issues in,
183-190
staff preparation for, 184-185
staff responsibilities in, 185-188
staff training for, preparation for,
188-189
taxation in, 81-84
telecommunications,
infrastructure of,
development of, 69
training for
approaches to, 189-190
methods of, 189-190
model for, 190
types of, 185
transformation of delivery in, 47
in a transinstitutional
environment, 5-24,
119-120
types of, 5
usage patterns of, 88-96
user power in, 96-101
RightPages, 126
Robotic stack cost per year, 89,90f

Sanville, T., 110
Schmidt, S., 28
Scholarly journals
changes needed in, 61-63
costliness of, impact of, 59-61
electronic delivery of, 61-63
importance of, 52-53
numbers of, 54

production of, changes needed in,
61-63
resource sharing related to, 63-64
subscribers of, 55
Scholarly publishing
copyright and, 49-52
history of, 53-54
of journals
growth of, 53-55
production of, steps in, 55
shortcomings in, 55-59. *See
also under* Journal
article
resource sharing related to, 63-64
shortcomings in, 55-59. *See also
under* Journal article
production of, steps in
Scholars' Express, 140
Scientific journals, costliness of, 60
Self-sufficiency, expanding resources
for, 12-15
SERHOLD, 123
Serials, expenditures for, 7
Sibley, J. L., 9
SilverPlatter databases, 173-174
Skills for resource sharing, 186-187
Special collections
collecting of, 17-18
founding of, 10
Special libraries, scholarly journals
in, 55
Springer Publishing Co., Red Sage
project in, 176
Standard generalized mark-up
language (SGML), 177
Standards Working Group, 196-197
State funding, of public universities,
28
Storage, costs of, vs. communication
costs, 86-88
Storage and retrieval costs, 88-89,
90f
Stubbs, K., 7
Swindler, L., 73-74

Tagged Image File Format (TIFF),
174-175
Taxation, as mechanism for resource
sharing, 81-84
Telecommunications infrastructure,
development of, 69
The Genuine Article (TGA), 140
The Mediterranean, 14
TIFF, 174-175
Training, in library partnerships,
183-184
Transinstitutional environment,
resource sharing in, 19-20
TULIP project, 176

UnCover Company, 100, 176
UnCover Reveal service, 173-174
University(ies), public
as centers of excellence, 32-33
challenges facing, 36-37
consortia in, 32
core services of, 33-34
funding to, 28
information technology and
distributed computing in,
35-36
partnering of, 29
and the public good, 27-37
redefinition of primary clientele
and consortial partnerships,
35
resource sharing in, future of,
31-36
resources for, reallocation of,
34-35
value-added services to, 34
University libraries
escalating costs to, 68-69
technological factors affecting,
68-70
*University Libraries and Scholarly
Communication*, 69
University LIcensing Program

(TULIP), with Elsevier
Science Publishers, 126
University of Georgia Libraries,
journal cost of, 59-60
University of Tennessee, Knoxville
(UTK) libraries, EJL in,
125
University of Vermont, funding to,
28
U.S. Copyright Act of 1976, 50
User power, 96-101

Value-added services
defined, 34
of document delivery services,
135
Vassar College, interlibrary loan at,
171
"Virtual Library," 44-45

Wegner, L. S., 8
Wilson Library Bulletin, 180
Working Group on Intellectual
Property Rights, 200
World War II, prosperity of libraries
following, 10-11

Z39.50 protocol, 146-149